Master Yo

Rewire Your Mind, Manage Your Feelings, Overcome Negativity, Reduce Anxiety, Stress, Anger, Worry, Develop Self-Control, and Live a Happier Life

Dr. Louise Lily Wain

© **Copyright 2019 - All rights reserved.**

The content contained within this book may not be reproduced, duplicated or transmitted without direct written permission from the author or the publisher.

Under no circumstances will any blame or legal responsibility be held against the publisher, or author, for any damages, reparation, or monetary loss due to the information contained within this book. Either directly or indirectly.

Legal Notice:

This book is copyright protected. This book is only for personal use. You cannot amend, distribute, sell, use, quote or paraphrase any part, or the content within this book, without the consent of the author or publisher.

Disclaimer Notice:

Please note the information contained within this document is for educational and entertainment purposes only. All effort has been executed to present accurate, up to date, and reliable, complete information. No warranties of any kind are declared or implied. Readers acknowledge that the author is not engaging in the rendering of legal, financial, medical or professional advice. The content within this book has been derived from various sources. Please consult a licensed professional before attempting any techniques outlined in this book.

By reading this document, the reader agrees that under no circumstances is the author responsible for any losses, direct or indirect, which are incurred as a result of the use of information contained within this document, including, but not limited to, — errors, omissions, or inaccuracies.

Table of Contents

Introduction

Chapter 1: Am I A Big Ball of Emotions?

  What Are Emotions?

  A Deeper Look at Our Basic Emotions

    Happiness

    Sadness

    Fear

    Anger

    Disgust

    Surprise

  How Emotions Are Created

    The Cannon-Bard Theory

    The James-Lange Theory

    The Schacter-Singer Model

  What Impact Do Your Emotions Have?

    Do Emotions Impact Our Health?

What About Our Minds and Bodies? Do Emotions Impact Those Too?

How Emotions Impact Your Performance at Work

Key Takeaway

Chapter 2: The Change That Comes from Within

How to Change Your Emotions

Using Your Emotions to Grow

How to Deal with Your Most Important Emotions

Bonus Tips to Help You Manage Your Emotions

Chapter 3: How Do the (Emotionally) Strong Survive?

Facts You Might Not Know About Emotions

How Mentally Strong People Control Their Emotions

Repercussions of Ignoring or Suppressing Your Emotions

Chapter 4: Doing Away with Negativity

How to Overcome Negativity

How to Reduce Anxiety

Am I Experience Anxiety? Or Just Worry?

Overcoming Anxiety

How to Minimize Stress, Anger, and Worry

Chapter 5: Master It, Control It, Be Happy About It

Steps to Master Your Emotions

   Step 1: Begin by Identifying What Emotions You Feel

   Step 2: Acknowledge and Appreciate

   Step 3: Analyze and Be Curious

   Step 4: Eliminate the "I'm A Victim" Mentality

   Step 5: Be Confident in Your Abilities

Building Your Emotional Resilience

Make It Your Personal Commitment to Change

Developing Self-Control to Live a Happier Life

   Definition of Self-Control

   But Why Is It So Hard to Develop?

   The Link Between Self-Control and Self-Esteem

   Steps to Building Your Happiness and Self-Control

Concluding Thoughts

Conclusion

Introduction

Congratulations on purchasing this book and thank you for doing so.

Learning about your emotions is a bold, daring move towards change—a change that not many others might be working on just because they haven't realized just how important this change could be to their lives.

You've decided that you want to take control of your life and learn how to master that one, powerful force that exists within us all, to conquer it so it no longer gets the best of you. You've decided that you want to learn how to master your emotions once and for all.

There are only two words that you need to take away as a final lesson by the time you reach the end of this book. *Emotions matter*. They are the very essence that determines whether we go on to live a happy life or a miserable one.

They are present in every aspect of our lives, at home, in our workplace, our friendships, our love life; relationships, family life, and almost every situation or circumstance is a potential opportunity to experience an emotion.

They make you behave in ways you ordinarily wouldn't, and they can even save the day in a difficult situation when you accurately read and learn to identify the type of emotions you're feeling.

There's a lot more to understanding your emotions that simply putting a name to an internal experience happening within you. Emotions are complex, and before you can even begin to control and regulate them, you need to first have a thorough understanding of what you're working with, which is what the goal of this book is going to be. To help readers get a better grasp of the concept of emotions and what they can do to your life. To broaden your understanding on the subject, which - given the important role that emotions play in all our lives - is the key to comprehending to what extent we are influenced by our emotions and what happens when we don't deal with them like we should.

Emotions can happen very quickly, and if you don't learn how to regulate them, they're going to overpower you and seize control over your actions. You'll be at the mercy of saying or doing the first impulsive reaction that comes to mind, spurred by your emotions.

Emotions can be helpful, but not if you overreact. When you don't have control over the cause of your emotional state, you will *never be in control*, no matter how you may try to convince yourself otherwise.

To minimize the destructive effects of your explosive emotional episodes requires a thorough understanding of not just your emotions, but of *yourself*.

At the end of the day, the thing that all of us want is to be happy. Everything that we say or do comes back to trying to achieve happiness.

Being happy is not such an impossible concept to grasp, not if you learn how to become the master of one of the most powerful forces within you—*your emotions*.

There are plenty of books on this subject on the market, thanks again for choosing this one! Every effort was made to ensure it is full of as much useful information as possible, please enjoy!

Chapter 1: Am I A Big Ball of Emotions?

Emotions rule our very existence. Well, not entirely, but they can if we allow them to. Emotions already have a big part to play in a lot of our everyday functioning.

We sometimes make decisions based on our emotions. We choose what we can to pursue based on our emotions. We even select the activities we want to be involved in based on the emotions that it invokes within us.

They play such a crucial role in our lives, yet how much do we understand about emotions?

What are they?

How are they formed?

Why do we experience these emotions and what impact do they have upon us? Or even the people around us?

What are emotions and why are they so powerful?

What Are Emotions?

That's a question, researchers have been trying to answer for a very long time. *Discovering Psychology,* a book published by authors Don and Sandra Hockenbury, revealed that the emotions we feel are rather complex, a psychological state which involves some very distinctive components. Three of them, to be exact, which are:

- The expressive response
- The experience we undergo subjectively

- The physiological response is invoked.

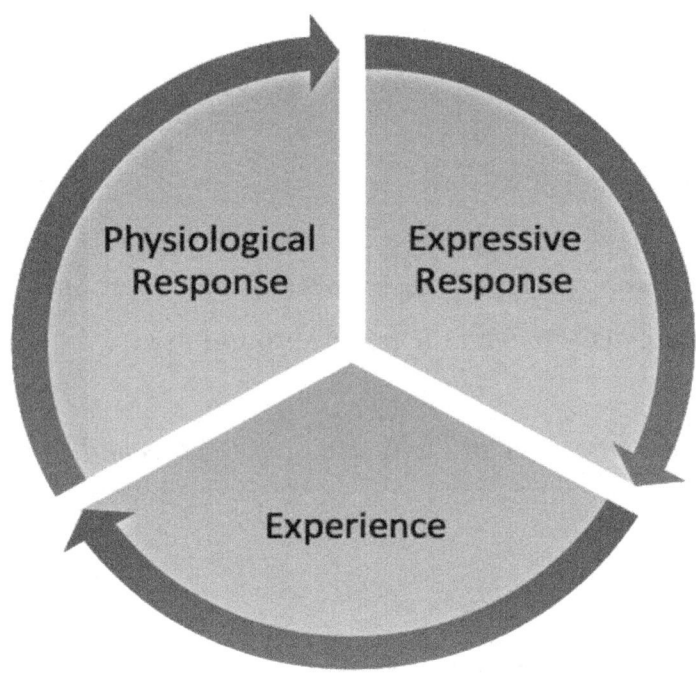

Components of Emotions

Psychologist Paul Eckman, back in 1972, put forth this idea that universally, we all experience six basic types of emotions that goes across cultures.

No matter who you are or where you may come from, the six emotions that are universally experienced by everyone in the world are happiness, anger, fear, sadness, disgust, and surprise.

However, Eckman later expanded his list in 1999 to include several emotions which were classified as basic emotions too. The list then included satisfaction, shame, embarrassment, contempt, pride, amusement, and excitement.

Professor Robert Plutchick, sometime around the 1980s, introduced what is known as the "Wheel of Emotions", which was a system used to classify emotions.

Plutchik's model showed how the various emotions we experienced, could sometimes, be combined together, and he went on to propose that there were primarily eight different emotional dimensions that we experienced:

- Happiness versus sadness
- Anger versus fear
- Surprise versus anticipation
- Trust versus disgust

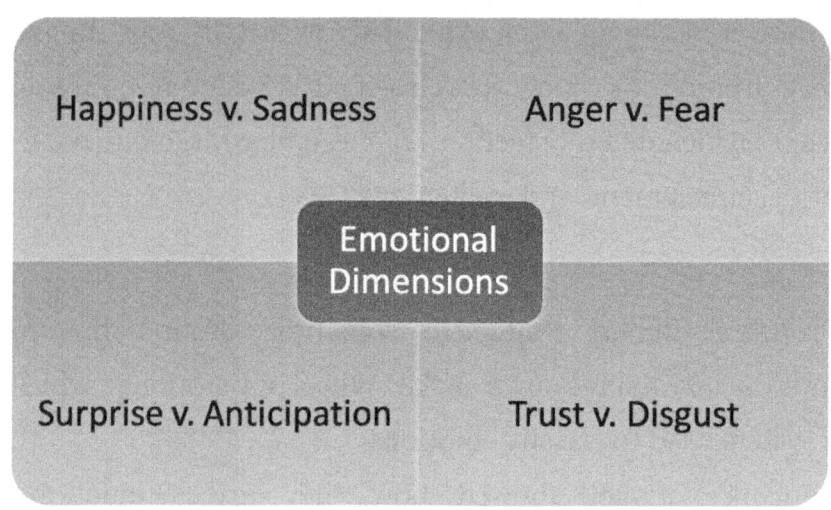

Plutchik's Emotional Dimension

According to Plutchik, these emotions could be combined, and when they were, they could create a whole host of new other emotions to be experienced. Happiness, for example, could be combined with anticipation and the resulting emotion could be excitement.

To get a better grasp of what emotions are, we need to go back to Eckman's three primary components and delve deeper into it:

- **The Expressive Response**

Which is also sometimes referred to as the behavioral response, this component is perhaps the most familiar of all because this is where emotions are expressed the way we know how.

We spend a huge amount of our time trying to decipher and accurately interpret the emotions of the people around us.

We try to guess what they might be going through, maybe even try to imagine being in their shoes. The ability to accurately comprehend our emotions, and that of others around us, is what psychologists refer to as emotional intelligence or EI, which plays a major role in body language communication.

- **The Experience We Undergo Subjectively**
Several experts on the subject believe that there are several emotions which are experienced at a universal level, regardless of where we hail from, and what our culture or background is.

However, researchers also believe that emotions are subjective. Emotions are generally classified using broad labels such as "happy" or "angry, but the way that you experience these emotions are subjective because they are multi-dimensional.

If you were experiencing anger for example, *what kind* of anger were you going through? Mild anger? Aggressive anger? Full on rage? Fury perhaps?

That is subjective, and because emotions are not always experienced in their purest forms, most of the time we find ourselves experiencing a mixture of emotions based on the situations we find ourselves in.

- **The Physiological Response**

Our physiological responses have a part of play in the emotions that we experience. When your heart seems to beat faster and palpate when you feel fear, or when you feel that lurch in your stomach each time you feel anxious, those emotions are brought on by a strong physiological reaction. This was explained by Philip Bard and Walter Cannon in their Cannon-Bard theory of emotion, which is sometimes referred to as the thalamic theory of emotion, too.

The Cannon-Bard theory explains that when we simultaneously feel strong emotions *and* have a physiological response at the same time, these could manifest themselves physically such as through trembling, the tension in the muscles, or even sweating.

That's the body's autonomic nervous system at work and the reason why some situations tend to trigger the fight or flight response within us. It's because of these autonomic responses.

More recently in 2017, an interesting study suggested that there were a lot more basic emotions that we experience than initially thought. 27 more emotions to be exact, although what researchers of the study discovered was that we experienced these emotions n a more gradient level, rather than distinct.

A Deeper Look at Our Basic Emotions

Taking a closer look at some of the common basic emotions every human goes through, it is intriguing to observe the various ways in which these emotions are expressed depending on the situation on the context.

Happiness

Take happiness, for example. One of the most basic emotions we all experience, which also happens to be the most sought after emotion universally.

Ask anyone what they want, and they'll tell you they want to be happy. Almost everything we do is based on the hope that it is going to make us happier. Why we strive to achieve this is because happiness is one of the most pleasant states of emotions that we experienced.

Words which are generally used to categorize this feeling include joy, contentment, satisfaction and even gratification.

The way this emotion is expressed is through body language, tone of voice and facial expression.

Since the 1960s, the amount of research being conducted on this emotion has increased rather substantially within several disciplines, including a branch now known as positive psychology.

Happiness on its own is an emotion which is universally experienced in the say way. The aspect that differs is what we *think* is going to make us happy, and this is subject to a lot of different influences.

In reality, the reasons for our happiness are subjective.

What makes one person happy might be different for someone else. Some people are happy chasing their careers to feel a sense of fulfillment, while others are happier concentrating on forging meaningful relationships instead.

Sadness

Another universal emotion is happiness' exact opposite. Sadness.

Characterized as an emotion that is transient, words used to depict this emotion include grief, disappointment, disheartened, disinterested or a sense of despair.

Just like happiness, we are all prone to going through this emotion every now and then, and we will continue to experience this several times in our lives.

Sadness, however, is an emotion which can be damaging to our physical and mental health. Prolonged and chronic levels of sadness can lead to mental health issues like depression and anxiety, which then leads to social isolation, withdrawal, and a feeling of disconnect.

Another reason why sadness can be a dangerous emotion (depending on what degree you're experiencing it), is because it can lead to dangerous coping habits to attempt to deal with the strong feelings you have within you. Self-medication, alcoholism, negative thoughts that turn you into a toxic individual.

Many that engage in such behavior believe that it is going to help, not realizing that in reality, it's only exacerbating their sadness and making things worse.

Fear

One of the more powerful emotions, and a big reason why early humans especially, managed to survive when they had to live in the wild.

Fear provokes you to take action when you believe you're under threat, or afraid of losing something valuable.

Fear is the primary trigger for the fight or flight response, a mechanism which is built within us all, even though we no longer have to rely on it so heavily for survival.

When we experience this emotion, the general symptoms that accompany it include rapid heart rate, tense muscles, and a mind that snaps to attention and becomes more alert.

Our bodies in this state are primed to either flee or stand our ground and face the perceived threat head-on. This emotion triggers the most visible physiological responses, although it is not experienced in the same way by everyone.

Unlike anger though, fear is one emotion that we can condition ourselves to overcome. Exposing ourselves repeatedly to the things that we're afraid of over time helps to build a tolerance or resilience towards that trigger until we no longer feel so afraid anymore.

Repeated exposure will cause your fear levels to decrease over time, which is then followed by a sense of accomplishment or pride at having overcome that fear.

Anger

A particularly powerful basic emotion is anger, often accompanied by several words used to describe the varying degrees of anger which we feel.

This includes hostile, annoyed, frustrated, furious and even feeling antagonistic towards someone.

Like fear, anger is another emotion that triggers the fight or flight response within us, and whenever we experience this emotion, we might be inclined to act in a way we believe is protecting ourselves.

It's easy to tell when someone is angry, especially through the powerful facial expressions that show through. Frowning, glaring, clenching of the fists, tightening of the jaw, snarling or pursing their lips into a thin line are all the visible signs of anger.

This emotion is even strong enough to trigger a physiological response, such as an increased heart rate, sweating or even turning red in the face with anger.

Just like sadness, anger can be a rather dangerous emotion, especially physically when it leads to aggressive behaviors which include hitting, kicking, punching and even throwing objects at another which could cause them physical harm.

Anger puts you, and everyone else around you in danger if left out of control.

The fact that people have been known to kill in their rage goes to show just how strong a reaction this emotion can invoke.

When expressed in unhealthy ways, anger can become a real problem.

Disgust

Eckman classified disgust as another universal emotion because we all experienced it.

Everyone has, at one point, turned away from or felt disgusted towards something or someone. Disgust, like fear, is another emotion that can invoke a strong physiological response within us.

Depending on how disgusted we feel, physical symptoms could include gagging, retching, wrinkling our noses in disgust accompanied by the curl of the upper lip, and even verbally expressing how disgusted we feel.

The sense of disgust that we feel could be triggered by several factors, among which include smell, taste or sight. Disgust can also be experienced on a moral level, when we disapprove of another's behavior or think that the type of activities they might be engaged in, are what we believe to be evil, distasteful or immoral.

Surprise

Possibly one of the emotions that are experienced on the briefest level is a surprise.

It's fleeting and usually lasts no more than a few minutes, sometimes even seconds.

The surprise is experienced when we're faced with something unexpected, and the physiological response that often follows is the startled response. Unlike the other emotions, surprise can either be pleasant, neutral or negative.

An unpleasant surprise, for example, usually doesn't feel good. Like when someone jumps out at you from behind.

A pleasant surprise would be when your family and friends surprise you with a birthday party.

Because it's often unexpected, being surprised can also trigger the fight or flight response, as being suddenly taken aback and trigger a burst of adrenaline in your body that tells you to either run or stay.

Basic Human Emotions

How Emotions Are Created

Scientists have come up with several ideas and theories on the subject of how emotions are formed, based on Eckman's three primary components which were talked about above.

Eckman and Plutchik were not the only ones who had theories about how our emotions were form, Cannon-Bard and a number of other theorists had their own ideas too.

The Cannon-Bard Theory

First came to fruition in 1927, and it was developed by two Harvard colleagues known as Water Cannon and Philip Bard.

Together, they formulated their theory based on how the human nervous system works to express the emotions that go on within us, and what they discovered was that we were capable of experiencing emotions without necessarily getting any kind of physical response or feedback from the chemical messengers.

Cannon and Bard then experimented on the theory, and it was discovered that messages get sent to two different places in the human brain simultaneously.

The first message gets sent to the part of the brain known as the cortex, which is where emotions are formulated.

The second message gets sent to the hypothalamus, which is the portion of our brain that controls our body's automatic responses.

The hypothalamus is the one that tells our bodies how to react by sending chemical messengers, which is why some emotions cause physical symptoms that include rapid breathing, sweating, crying and shaking with fear or anger.

The James-Lange Theory

Though, came 40 years before Cannon and Bard proposed their theory.

The James-Lange theory was proposed by two scientists, the first being an American named William James and the second by a Danish man named Carl Lange.

Both scientists were committed to studying emotions and the kind of physical changes they evoke in the body, and what the relationship between these two factors was.

Sometime in 1885, both men proposed their own independent viewpoints, that emotions were based on two things.

The first was the changes we experienced physically, and the second was how well we understood these changes.

Both James and Lange were of the belief that we experienced these physical symptoms first, *after* which we would interpret its meaning. This is what created emotion.

However, there were two problems with the James-Lange theory. For one thing, emotions happened a little too quickly for chemical messengers to account for it. Secondly, some emotions have been known to trigger the same types of responses.

The Schacter-Singer Model

Was introduced in 1962, this time by two American scientists, Stanley Schacter and Jerome Singer.

Both decided to take elements from the Cannon-Bard and James-Lange theory, and then modify this in the hopes of better explaining what the relationship between our emotions and the physical responses we experienced were.

The Schacter-Singer model proposed the idea the physical changes we experienced as a result of an emotional reaction were the way we consciously needed to mentally process the emotion. Under this model, Schacter and Singer hoped to explain why some of the physical reactions we experience can be triggered by different types of emotions. That it is our brains which were helping us to decide what an appropriate response should be.

But *why do we need to have these emotions?*

What purpose do they serve?

There are some scientists who believe that emotions are part of the fundamental traits we associate with as being part of the overall human experience.

These emotions help to color our lives, helping us to differentiate the different situations we go through. Other scientists seem to believe that our emotions tend to serve as a motivation that helps us decide who we should behave.

What Impact Do Your Emotions Have?

Whatever the reason they may have been triggered, if there's one thing that we can be sure of it is this: *emotions help us survive.*

When you experience fear of getting knocked down by a car that's zooming past you as an attempt to cross the road, that fear causes you to freeze where you are, look both ways and only wait to cross the road when you know that it's safe.

Emotions also help you monitor the way you behave socially and adjust your responses to better suit your interaction with others. When you want to make a good impression on a potential business partner, you refrain from being overly emotional because you want to create a good first impression.

Our emotions exist for a reason, and that reason is that they matter.

All the ups and downs that we feel, the happiness, anger, sadness, joy, fear, nervousness and more, they are all a part of what makes us uniquely human.

Without these emotions, our human experiences wouldn't be the same and not nearly as exciting or colorful. We sometimes forget our emotions are a powerful force that is capable of turning our lives upside down if we don't regulate them the way that we should.

So powerful in fact, that our emotions don't just affect us, but the people around us too.

The way that we react based on emotions comes with consequences, and sometimes those consequences are not limited to just you alone.

Emotions have a way of influencing our minds and our bodies. Some emotions can be so powerful and consuming that they prevent us from thinking rationally or clearly.

American Nobel Laureate Herbert Simon even talked about how must understand the kind of role emotions play in rationality if we hope to understand it.

Dr. Simon reinforced that our emotions are capable of influencing, and sometimes even skewing our perception, which determines the outcome of a lot of the decisions we are faced with making in a day.

Making a decision when you're in a highly emotional state and it could quickly turn into a mistake.

It is nearly impossible to make logical, objective and rational decisions when we're in a highly emotional state, and because of that, emotions have a huge impact on our decision-making process.

Scientists have further confirmed this by agreeing that when emotions are involved, we are completely and utterly ineffective when it comes to making decisions.

In an office setup, emotions are not just going to impact you, but the people that you work with too.

Being emotional is not going to just impact your workload alone, and this is among the biggest reasons why recent research has discovered that one of the strongest contributing predictors to the success a person achieves at work comes down to emotional intelligence. When problems come up and decisions need to be made as a team, emotions are likely to collide.

That's not to say emotions are entirely bad, a little bit of emotion can sometimes be a good thing. It stops us from making decisions that are completely cold and heartless. It motivates us to take action and drives us to find solutions.

It's only when too much emotion is involved in these decisions that it starts to become a problem.

Do Emotions Impact Our Health?

Absolutely. It's referred to as "powerful" for a reason, and negative emotions are especially dangerous since they have been directly linked to numerous health-related problems already.

Being in a state of frequent emotional turmoil can lead to stress, which as we all know, is never good for the body. The elevated cortisol levels, adrenaline pumping through our veins, these are referred to as "stress hormones", and when they course through our bodies, they're pumping us up to react in a way that is quick and strong.

In the days of the early humans, these stress hormones would aid in their survival. Although today we don't need it to run away from the dangers of being eaten or attacked by an animal, stress hormones still emit the same powerful reaction and triggers, except that this time, it's done within different settings and contexts.

The fight or flight response has been mentioned a few times up to this point, and that's because it is one of the biggest impacts we experience as a result of these emotions.

That burst of adrenaline can lead to incredible feats of superhuman strength, and we find ourselves doing things we ordinarily wouldn't be able to.

In some ways, having a short burst of adrenaline and stress hormones can be a good thing, but once these stress triggers start to diminish and shut down, there's a good chance that the release of other chemicals which are needed to support some of our important bodily functioning, get shut down too.

Our bodies are incredible, but there's only so much they can handle at any given time, case in point being able to handle only impact at a time. In other words, our bodies can accept only one of two modes at any given time. We're either in the fight or flight response mode, or the healing and growth mode. One of the other.

Despite what you may believe, it is *not a norm* to be living in a constant state of stress. You may think that it can't be helped, or that's just how your life is and stress is a part of it, but this is not how we were meant to live.

Stress can have a tremendously negative impact on our bodies, not just physically, but emotionally too. On an emotional level, feeling stress and other negative emotions can result in irritability, feeling depressed and worthless, loss of purpose in life and loneliness.

We start to feel isolated—like nobody understand what we're going through—we become withdrawn, feel a sense of loneliness and eventually start to feel depressed because of all the imagined worries we are carrying about on our shoulders.

That's the kind of impact negative emotions can have on our minds.

On a physical level, certain emotions can leave an impact that includes side effects like weight gain, insomnia, chronic fatigue and muscular aches. Yet, many people tend to brush it off and not think twice about the connection between these symptoms and emotions, not realizing how this behavior pattern and way of thinking of is having damaging effects on their health.

What about Our Minds and Bodies? Do Emotions Impact Those Too?

Chronic illnesses like depression have been linked to poor mental health, which is often directly related to poor regulation of emotions.

Experiencing these unhealthy emotions over a long term period then leads to chronic illnesses, such as heart disease, diabetes, and even a stroke, and this was according to a 2013 article which was published in the *Primary Care Companion for CNS Disorders*.

Another study found that people had a 41% chance of depression and diabetes, so yes; it is safe to say emotions can have a rather significant impact on the state of our health without the proper regulation and management techniques.

A 2017 study even revealed the possible link between depression and its effect on our immune system, and that habits which were associated with depression - including a lack of sleep and physical activity - could potentially increase your chances of contracting more illnesses.

There is also the link between longevity and depression, which - according to a 2014 review - associated several mental health conditions with higher mortality rates.

Another 2017 study suggested that those who dealt with depression may be at risk of shorter lifespans, ranging anywhere from 7 years to 18 years shorter than the average human lifespan.

It cannot be denied that living in a state of constant emotional stress is eventually going to take its toll, and your health will be the one that ends up paying the price.

How Emotions Impact Your Performance at Work

A happy employee is a productive employee.
No one can get a job done well if they're feeling upset, distraught, angry, frustrated or any other highly emotional state which is going to impact their ability to think clearly and focus on the task at hand.

Economists at the University of Warwick discovered in a study that when employees were happy, it resulted in a 12% spike in their productivity levels at the office.

That's because when you're happy, you're naturally motivated to do more, no matter what task you've been assigned.

Whether it's at work or even a personal errand that you need to run, when you're happy and experiencing a flow of positive emotions, your motivation levels increase and along with it, the quality of your work.
A happy employee is able to produce a well-written report because of their increased ability to focus.

When they're not distracted by their emotions, their minds are concentrated on what they're doing.

Happy employees are also less likely to experience any side effects or symptoms that are invoked by negative emotions, such as frequent headaches, higher blood pressure, gastritis issues and more, all of which tend to affect productivity levels.

We spend a lot of our waking hours at the office more than we do at home, and it is important that emotions are regulated so we are better prepared to handle the different emotional scenarios we may experience as we go about our working day.

Learning how to handle these bouts of negative emotions can be a delicate matter. Since the workplace is a professional environment, being highly emotional is something that is frowned upon.
Despite how you feel, there's a certain expectation to handle yourself in a composed and acceptable manner.

Emotions can be highly infectious, and the next time there's a gloomy, or angry employee at work, make a quick observation about how this affects the people that the employee work with directly.

An employee who is always highly emotional is someone who can never be viewed as or even considered a leader. If this is a position that you aspire to find yourself in one day, being emotional is going to negatively impact your ability to turn that goal into a reality.

Since it is mostly negative emotions that tend to have the biggest impact on our performance and productivity, learning to recognize the most common emotions experienced in a work setting is the first step towards learning how to manage those emotions so they don't end up managing you.

- **Anger** is a common emotion that is experienced, and sometimes it is unavoidable.
  Some work environments - depending on the job you do - tend to be a place where tensions and stress levels run high. This could be a result of conflicts among colleagues and managers, feelings of frustration when things aren't getting done as they should. Even resentment when you see some of your colleagues being given preferential treatment. This is a dangerous emotion to have since it could lead to unwanted emotional outbursts when you least expect it, and in the worst case scenario would be you quitting your job in the heat of the moment.

- **Guilt** is an emotion that a lot of employees are wrecked with.
  You feel guilty in a group project when you feel like you're not pulling your weight enough.
  You feel guilty when you're not able to deliver on a task that you promised. You feel guilty about being involved in a gossip session about another colleague who happens to be a friend.

You feel guilty when you have to say no to a colleague that needed your help because your hands were already full.

There are a lot of scenarios in which an employee could experience guilt, and you might say that this emotion is sometimes unavoidable given the dynamics of having to work with multiple personalities less than one roof.

- **Jealousy or Envy** is to be expected in the workplace.
Not every colleague is going to be happy for your success, especially if they believe they deserve it more than you do. The reality is, in some workplace settings, rewards are not always doled out in a fair manner, which can then invoke a lot of unhappy emotions within you.
When you're feeling jealous or envious, those emotions could end up impacting your relationship with your colleague.
You might not want to speak to them, and they would be confused about your sudden change in attitude.
It's never a pleasant scenario to be in, and when other colleagues start to sense your hostility, it makes them uncomfortable and productivity levels eventually drop.

- **Fear** might not seem like a common emotion at work, but it is present among almost every employee.

There exists within everyone a fear of losing their job, an uncertainty which causes them to worry and constantly stay on the lookout for possible new opportunities instead of remaining loyal to the company that they're with.

But that's not the only thing that's inciting fear at the workplace.

There is also genuine fear when your manager or supervisor at work happens to be a nasty individual and a bully.

They make it very hard to work when you're always on your toes wondering when the next time your manager is going to jump on you and bully you into taking on an assignment you may not have the time to commit to.

Key Takeaway

Emotions are a force that is strong within all of us.

It is because of this very power that we need to learn how to master them once and for all.

To learn how to be the one who is in control, no matter what circumstances you may find yourself under.

To remain calm, composed and able to think rationally and make sound decisions is the mark of an emotionally mature person, and that's what the next few chapters are going to aim to focus on.

Chapter 2: The Change That Comes from Within

You're doing a wonderful job so far. You've already made a difference by making the decision to learn to master your emotions, understanding what they are, how they affect your lifestyle and what you can do to make a change for the better.

The next strategy is going to focus on how you can sidestep your emotional triggers by changing your emotions and using them to help you grow instead.

How to Change Your Emotions

Change is something that rarely ever comes easy. When you're trying to change what is part of your personality, the very thing that makes you human, and something that has been part of your life for so long, it's going to be even more of a challenge.

That's okay, because the best things in life are the things which are worth fighting and struggling for, and in this case, learning how to master your emotions is something you're going to fight for because it promises you a much better life.

A happier life, not just for you, but for the people you love. Emotional triggers will always be there because you don't exist in this world alone. You constantly have to interact with people, and even find yourself in situations that are less than ideal. It is bound to happen every now and then.

These factors are sometimes beyond your control, but there is something that you *can* control. You can control how you decide to respond. You *can make a conscious effort* to change your emotions, although it will take a lot of willpower to resist the urge to rise to the occasion and succumb to the temptation to react to what's provoking you.

It's going to be hard because you're going to have to go against your first instinctive response, to mindfully force yourself to react in a different way. A better way.

Changing your emotions may not be easy, but it is possible if you:

- **Choose to Do Something That Makes You Happy**
  Those who struggle with their emotions are often unhappier than most, which makes it very hard to hold onto any kind of happiness.

  When you're in a constant state of unhappiness, learning how to control anything becomes a challenge, let alone learning how to control something as powerful as your emotions.

  Learning to master your emotions is not just about getting it under control; it is about reconnecting with yourself too and finding your happiness once more.

  The best way to do that is to do something that makes you happy.

When you find yourself in an emotional situation and you're struggling to get a hold of yourself, walk away and choose instead to do something that makes you happy.

Each time you actively try to engage in an activity which brings you joy you'll find your negative emotions ebbing away quicker with each effort you make.

Harness the all-consuming power of happiness, because it's a good kind of emotion which will benefit you and everyone else around you.

A happier state of mind also makes it much easier for you to think with clarity, and in doing so, gives you a much better handle at controlling your emotions.

Do more of what makes you

HAPPY

- **Choose to Focus on The Solutions**

  Focus on the solution, not the problem.

  The force of the emotions that we feel can still manage to get the better of us, even when we're trying hard to reel them in.

  It is especially difficult because you're now trying to change the pattern of behavior that you have been used to for so long. The more you focus on the problem, the harder it is going to be to control your emotions, which is why you need to do the opposite.

  Instead of focusing on the problems, turn your attention to the solution instead.

  When emotions are running high, it is easy for someone else's anger, frustration or any other emotion they may be experiencing to rub off on you (emotions are contagious, remember?), and this will disrupt your own attempts at trying to master your emotions.

  It helps to focus on the situation at hand to help you find a solution to the problem.

The challenge here would be trying not to lose sight of the real issue that you should be focusing on.

When faced with an emotional situation or person, remind yourself that there must be a reason for it, and you need to find out what that reason is before you can attempt to find a solution for it.

Instead of thinking *"I'm so angry"* or *"I am furious"*, think about *"What can I do to resolve this"* instead.

There's always a reason and a trigger for every emotional outburst and getting to the root cause of it is how to try to resolve the problem.

> "Identify your problems but give your power and energy to solutions"
>
> — Anthony Robbins

- **Choose Not to Follow the Crowd**

    When everyone else is feeling emotionally charged up, it's not going to help matters in any way if you join the crowd and add fuel to the fire.

    Instead, try an alternative solution where you are the one who continues to remain calm instead. Allow yourself to be the one who keeps a cool head on their shoulders and take on the role of problem solver instead.

    It's easy to let the emotions of others affect you, but the beauty of this situation is that you *always have a choice*, and you need to remember that.

    If you *choose not to follow the crowd*, you're choosing to change your emotions. You now have the opportunity to provide that kind of solution for someone else.

> "Those who follow the crowd usually get lost in it"
>
> — Rick Warren

- **Choose A Time Out When You Need It**

    We all need a little space every now and then, especially when dealing with a highly emotional situation.

    If you're the emotional one, don't hesitate to ask for a time out or a break if you need to remove yourself from the situation and take a few minutes to calm yourself down.

    This is how you change your emotions, by choosing not to feed into it even more and taking a step back so you have a chance to breathe for a minute and try to calm your thoughts.

    Emotions cloud your judgment and stop you from thinking straight, and you will be no good to anyone if you can't even think straight because you're too focused on how you're feeling to care about anything else.

The best thing you could do to provide a helpful solution would be to get some space if you feel like you need it. Recommend that they get some space too, so everyone can come back and revisit the issue when they're not as worked up emotionally and willing to listen to reason.

There are times and a place for effective communication and being emotional is neither the right time nor place. Take a time out if you need one.

- **Choose Open and Welcoming Body Language Responses**

Another challenging exercise in self-control and self-regulation is going to be making a conscious decision to remain calm, open and welcoming with your body language, despite the strong emotional situation you may find yourself in.

Adopt body language mannerisms which are inviting and you'll have a much better shot at getting your emotions under control quickly.

Body language is just as powerful as the words that you speak, and sometimes you could even end up making the situation worse without ever having said a word.

When someone is being emotional in front of you for example, and you roll your eyes and shake your head, you could end up aggravating the situation and making things worse, even if you never uttered a word the whole time.

As challenging as it may be, body language is just as important trying to resolve social problems which are caused by emotions.

What you need to do to change those emotions is to adopt open and welcoming body language gestures, which include making good eye contact, not crossing your arms in front of your chest, not frowning, clenching or muscles or display any visible indication that you may be feeling emotional yourself.

> "Emotion always has its roots in the unconscious and manifests itself in the body"
>
> — Irene Claremont de Castillejo

- **Choose to Talk to Someone**

    We'll talk more about the negative effects of trying to suppress your emotions, but for now, one method of learning to keep your emotions under control is to talk to someone about it when it starts to feel like it might be too much.

    Instead of keeping all those emotions bottled up inside you with no healthy means of release; choose instead to talk to a friend or family member with whom you're comfortable with.

    Venting, as it is often referred to, can make you feel much better, almost like a weight has been lifted off your shoulders.

When that weight is gone, your head feels much clearer and changing your emotions then becomes easier.

Friends or family members who know you well enough might be able to provide some form of insight too and even give you their feedback which could prove to be useful advice.

Using Your Emotions to Grow

Your emotions can do one of two things.

They can either help you grow and become a better version of yourself, or it can hold you back and destroy your reputation.

The former open doors to new and greater opportunities, while the latter will leave you with a reputation that you're someone others should stay away from when you're unstable and emotional.

To achieve the former, you need to begin cultivating a positive environment for yourself, one that is going to make it easier to nurture these positive emotions and help you grow.

Here's the twist - *it's not all about you*. That's right, growing your emotions is not going to be an exercise that is entirely focused on you.

This time, you're going to be focused on making others around you feel good, which in turn helps you feel good.

Humans are social creatures by nature, and doesn't it always feel much better when you know you've done something that makes a positive difference in someone else's life other than yourself?

That's how you use your emotions to grow as a person. This is what you need to do:

- **Be Appreciative**

    There is nothing that demotivates you and other people around you quicker than a lack of appreciation.

    Showing a little gratitude and appreciation every now and then can go a long way towards turning your emotions around. When you're feeling terrible after a long day, just remembering that there's a lot in your life to be grateful for despite all that is enough to put a smile on your face.

Simple phrases like "thank you" or "nice job", maybe even a "we couldn't have done it without you" can make a real difference in your moral and that of others you spend your time with.

> "Social scientists have found that the fastest way to feel happiness is to practice gratitude."
>
> — Chip Conley

- **You Need to Be Engaging**

No matter whom you interact with, be engaging and go the extra mile to make a connection with them.

A genuine human connection is what we all long for deep down inside, and there's no one who is ever going to tell you that they enjoy being lonely.

No matter who you're engaging with, build a connection that is meaningful. With family, friends, and colleagues, out to them on a regular basis, congratulate them on little victories accomplished, and remember special moments like their birthdays and anniversaries.

These efforts will go a long way towards keeping the people who matter happy, and in turn, you will feel a lot happier too.

- **Making Others Feel Like They Matter Too**
You're not the only one who wants to feel like you matter.

Others want the same thing. If this approach was practice more in the workplace, it would make such a difference to morale and productivity levels for all employees involved.

There are going to be some people in your team that have better ideas than the next person, it happens. Instead of feeling jealous or envious, why not feel happy for them for a change?

If you wish it had been you, then use that as motivation to work even harder so you're ready for the next opportunity that comes along.

Make it your personal policy to encourage anyone with an idea to approach you and give them a chance to express their ideas.

This kind of empathy and understanding is a sign of emotional maturity on your part, and that is always a good thing. It means you've grown.

> "People will forget what you said, people will forget what you did, but people will never forget how you made them feel"
>
> — Maya Angelou

- **Be Trustworthy**

If you want to be thought of as someone who is positive and approachable, you need to be someone who is trustworthy.

Without trust, there is no possibility of working together well. When others feel like they can't trust you, it's impossible for them to be themselves around you, let alone consider any kind of relationship with you, personal or professional.

It is easy, to be honest when the news that you intend to share is good.

It takes courage to be even more honest when the news that you have to share is bad news.

- **Choosing Politeness**

It is so easy to start yelling, screaming and throwing about some verbally abusive words when your emotions are out of control.

When someone is attacking you verbally, your natural instinct might be to start defending yourself and fighting back.

Trying to remain polite and professional is going to be the last thing on your mind, but it is what you must do if you want to use your emotions as an opportunity to grow instead.

If you continue to keep your tone calm, polite and civil throughout the emotional situation, sooner or later, others will follow suit.

Choosing to remain polite when someone is being extremely emotional in your face is not a sign of weakness on your part.

You're not allowing yourself to be taken advantage of, you're making the choice not to stoop down to their level, and that is a reflection on your character.

> "What wisdom can you find that is greater than kindness?"
>
> — Jean-Jacques Rousseau

- **Change Your Thoughts to Change Your World**

A beautiful quote by Norman Vincent Peale which sums up perfectly that the only way to use your emotions to help you grow is to first change your perspective and your thoughts.

Reflecting upon his words, you'll come to see just how powerful the nature of the thoughts that we have in our mind can be.

Our thoughts can determine whether we're happy, sad, feeling optimistic, positive, frustrated, resentful, angry, bitter, or negative.

If you want to live a life that is happy, a life that is filled with contentment and a sense of fulfillment, then one thing's for sure, and that is you need to change your thought patterns.

If you want to use your emotions to help you grow, you need to change the way that you think about them. It begins with getting rid of your excuses.

To keep your emotions under control, you're going to have to get rid of all your excuses. No more making excuses that justify your behavior. No more finding excuses and reasons to justify your poor emotional reactions and outbursts.

Learning from your mistakes is what people who grow to become better versions of themselves do.

Excuses are the kind of thought patterns that will hold you back the longer you hold onto them, like an anchor that just weighs you down and prevents you from moving on.

> "Very little is needed to make a happy life; it is all within yourself, in your way of thinking."
>
> — Marcus Aurelius

- **Make Your Own List**

    Create a little list for yourself where you write down all the changes that you want to see happening in your life from this point forward.

    Having it visually represented in front of you makes it stick in your mind for much longer. This old-school trick is still among the most effective techniques that have managed to stick around for one, very simple reason.

It works. Write down all the goals that you want to accomplish by the end of this master your emotions journey.

A simple goal with a clear outline of how your thought pattern needs to change to accomplish it.

Whenever you feel like managing your emotions is a particular struggle at any point during this process, simply look at the list again to renew your resolve and remind yourself as to why you're doing this.

- **Learning to Let Go**

Next to forgiveness, learning to let go of the past and move on is the next biggest indicator of emotional maturity.

A sign that you have grown from the person you used to be. Those who have been struggling for a long time with trying to keep their emotions under control will tell you this is one of the hardest steps to accomplish. Replaying or holding onto past hurts or mistakes is going to do nothing except get you emotionally worked up for nothing.

Now that we know emotions can have both physical and psychological effects on our wellbeing (and not in a good way), it then becomes more important than ever that you learn how to let things go.

Your very health depends on it. It may seem impossible, but you'll be happy to know that learning how to let things go is a trait which can be learned over time.

Everything can be learned, you just need to be willing *to learn.*

> "The truth is, unless you let go,
> unless you forgive yourself,
> unless you forgive the situation,
> unless you realize that
> the situation is over,
> you cannot move forward."
> — Steve Maraboli

- **Be the Forgiving One**

   Life would be so much simpler if we could all just get along and no one got emotionally out of control. In a perfect world, that would be the ideal scenario.

Once you have learned how to let go of your negative emotions and the things that bother you, there's one more aspect involved with learning how to use your emotions to help you grow.

You need to learn to forgive.

This is going to be equally as challenging, perhaps even more so, because forgiveness is not something that comes easy to many.

Learning how to calm your emotions probably the easier thing to do.

Forgiveness is decidedly harder, but it is a necessary part of the process towards your overall journey to mastering your unhealthy emotions if you want to grow and become the better person you know you can be.

> "Forgive others,
> not because
> they deserve forgiveness,
> but because
> you deserve peace"
>
> — Jonathan Lockwood Huie

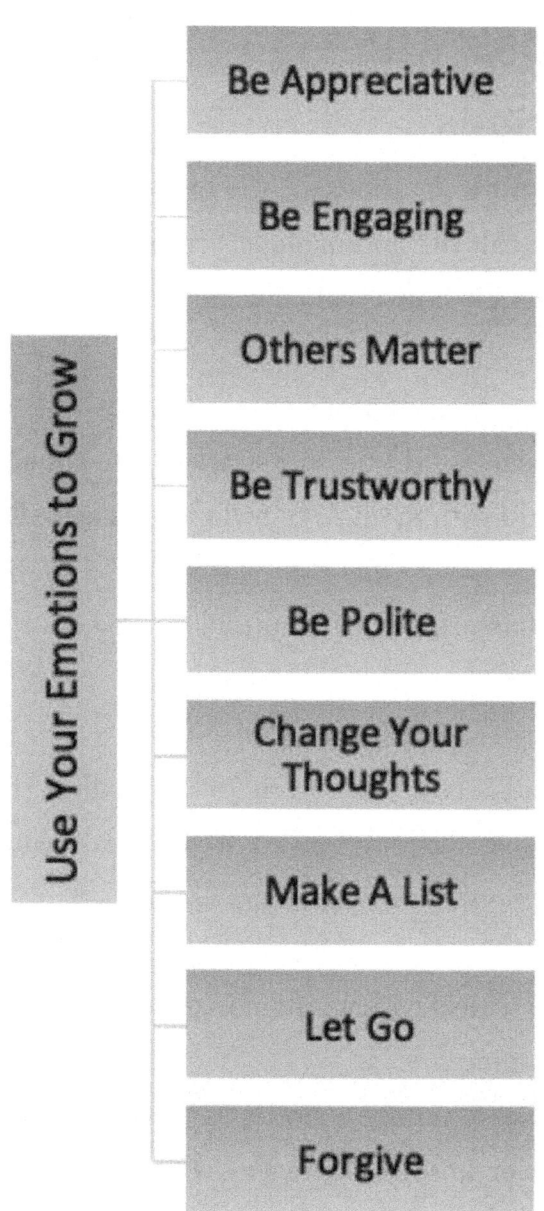

How to Use Your Emotions to Grow

How to Deal with Your Most Important Emotions

Your most important emotions, the ones you want to learn how to effectively deal with and manage, are any emotion that is going to cause a negative impact on your life.

Since these are the emotions that often get out of control the most, your focus should be on mastering the coping mechanism to help you deal with them so they don't end up ruling your life.

The road to mastering your emotions can be a long, sometimes difficult process.

Some may find it easier than others. Regardless, the highs and lows that you go through need to be dealt with since they significantly impact your wellbeing.

Learning how to deal with your emotions will impact how you are perceived by others.

When you see a highly emotional person who is prone to outbursts, never knowing when or where they might suddenly explode, how do you perceive them?

Are they someone you want to be around? Highly unlikely, since you're going to have to always be on your toes around this type of individual.

You never know when you can let your guard down, and that can be an exhausting experience. If you don't want others to think of you this way, you need to learn how to manage your emotions, particularly the negative ones since they leave the strongest repercussions.

Some people are a lot more temperamental than others which would explain why they get emotional a lot quicker and more frequently.
Let's take a look at some of the potential reasons behind why you find yourself losing control of your emotions more often than you should.

It could be attributed to several factors:

- **You're Easily Stressed**
  You can't even remember a moment when you were not feeling stressed.

No one can blame you. These are hectic times that we live in, so much so that feeling relaxed and calm most of the time has become a rare commodity.

Stress could also act as a potential trigger for your emotions too, leading to abrupt outbursts, temper tantrums, and irrational behavior.

It is your body's way of reacting to the stress that you already feel, and it's unfortunate that it causes you to lose control over the situation while you do it.

- **It Depends on Your Temperament**
We are all different and therefore, our personalities and our temperaments are different.

Not all of us are wired the same way. Some act quicker, while others need more time to process their next move. Some people just happen to be a lot more emotional than others because that's their temperament.

- **You Grew Up Among Emotional People**
The role models you had growing up have an impact on shaping you to become the person you are today.

If you were surrounded by family members who were very emotional people, chances are this has influenced you to some degree.

When this is all that you knew growing up, you're not going to see anything wrong with it until it's been pointed out to you.

You don't know any other way because this is how you were raised.

- **Your Perception About Life**

Are you an optimist or a pessimist? Does seeing the bright side of a bleak situation something that comes easily to you?

Or do you have a rather cynical, hostile view of the world around you?

The glass is always half empty and there is not a silver lining in sight.

When things don't work out the way that you expect them to, it sets off your emotions and you start to feel like you're spiraling out of control.

Your perception and view on life are going to impact the way you manage your emotions and your ability to remain calm even in situations you don't always have control over.

- **Your Communication Skills Need Work**

  The inability to express yourself effectively can be frustrating. A lot of people fail to realize this, and they don't connect poor emotional management with poor communication skills.

  When you have a hard time making yourself understood, or expressing yourself, it can often lead to a lot of feelings of frustration.

  Poor communication skills can often lead to a lot of misunderstanding, which could lead to arguments which cause you to feel emotional.

Not all emotions need to be regulated. If you're already exhibiting the proper emotional response that is appropriate to the situation you find yourself in, that's acceptable already.

It is only when your emotions are inappropriate that you need to start stepping in with the right management techniques and learn how to express yourself in another way.

The most important thing to begin with, however, is to learn how to first remain calm in any situation.

Staying calm buys you the crucial few minutes that you need to quickly assess the situation and gauge if your emotional response is an appropriate one.

Fortunately, it is easy to control most emotions, or eventually learn how to control them so they no longer remain in the driver seat.

With practice and time, everyone can learn how to deal with and manage their emotions, and to give yourself your best chance of doing so, preparation ahead of time is the key:

- **Choosing Your Situation**

    If you know a situation is going to trigger an emotional response from you, avoid it at all costs.

    Do your best to stay away from it, especially if you know ahead of time that it's coming.

Let's look at this example, where you know getting caught in traffic causes a lot of negative emotions, try to leave 10 or 15 minutes earlier from your home to avoid the unnecessary burden of dealing with these emotions, which are likely going to affect your mood for the rest of the day.

- **Acknowledge, Don't Deny**
Denying your emotions or trying to suppress them is one of the worst things you could do.

This is not going to help you learn to control it. Facing your emotional demons may not be something that you want to do but living in denial and ignoring it never solved anything either.

To learn how to deal with it, you must first acknowledge that there is something that needs to be done about it. The more you deny your emotions, the worse it will be for you when it comes to managing it.

- **Deliberate Calmness**
Emotions can get the best of you, which is why learning to deliberately slow down your thoughts and emotions can go a long way towards helping you learn how to control and effectively deal with them.

Do you notice that when you start to feel emotional (negatively emotional), your thoughts begin to race and get muddled up?

Your breathing quickens and it becomes difficult to keep a clear head and you react based on your impulses instead?

What you need to do now is to practice slowing your thoughts down, to make sure that you are in control at every step of the way. This can be achieved through practice.

- **Make Adjustments**

   If you can't avoid the situation entirely, make adjustments and modifications to it so you still maintain the upper hand over your emotions.

   These modifications need to be based on the kind of emotion you're trying to deal with or minimize. Like disappointment, for example. If you were trying to avoid disappointment over missing a movie you've been waiting to watch for so long, trying to arrange your schedule so all your affairs are in order and your schedule is kept as clear as possible on the day of the movie premiere.

Even if something last minute comes up, you'll still have time to deal with it because you've adjusted your schedule and kept it clear of any pressing or urgent matters.

Find solutions to minimize the emotions you're trying to avoid, there's always a solution to every problem—you just have to spend enough time thinking about it and planning for it.

- **Distract Yourself**

Focusing on the situation that caused you to feel emotional in the first place is only going to make things worse.

The more you think about it, the more emotional you're going to become.

All common sense just seems to go out the window in the heat of the moment. You need to distract yourself, that's the only way you're going to buy yourself enough time to calm down and get under control again.

Deflect your attention elsewhere until you've forgotten about what it was that was threatening to derail your control over your emotions.

You need to distance yourself from the triggers for as long as it takes until you are properly distracted enough until the situation no longer bothers you.

- **Mindful Breathing**

    They use this technique all the time in meditation.

    Mindful breathing is a useful exercise to have on hand when you're faced with the possibility of losing control of your emotions.

    Whenever you're under stress and feeling angry for instance, do you notice how your breathing becomes shallow and more ragged?

    By learning a few effective breathing techniques, you can dramatically control your response to a situation or a person.

    Mindful breathing is an exercise that takes practice and it something which is simple and easy to do right. You should aim to practice this exercise often until you are able to see a difference in the way that you react to situations.

    Breathe deeply in and out, slow and steady, focus on each inhale and exhale. Focus on the air that is flowing in and out of your body. Breathe in deeply through your nose, and exhale slowly through your mouth.

This repetitive exercise will help you relax, remain calm and learn to be in control of your breathing patterns.

Bonus Tips to Help You Manage Your Emotions

Since emotions can be challenging for all of us, a few additional strategies come in handy as you work on learning how to master your emotions, rewire your mind and manage your feelings.

Developing self-control begins with learning how to effectively manage your emotions, and if you're finding it a challenge to change your thought patterns and the way that you react, the following affirmations will help you through the process and remind you that you can do this:

- *I will not allow my emotions to get the best of me; I am in control every day.*
- *I am in control of my thoughts and reactions.*
- *I always have a choice to respond the right way.*
- *I am capable of learning how to control my emotions because I can do anything I set my mind too.*
- *Emotions are temporary; they will not get the best of me.*
- *I realize I am emotional right now. I accept, embrace it, and I will do my best to calm down.*
- *Today is going to be a good day. I will not let my emotions get out of control today.*

- *Every day I am getting better at controlling my emotions, every day I am stronger.*
- *I have more control over my emotions than I realize.*
- *Today, I CHOOSE to be in control of my emotions no matter what comes my way.*

Chapter 3: How Do the (Emotionally) Strong Survive?

Here's an interesting fact about emotions that you might not have known.

In the old days, ancient doctors once believed the various organs in our bodies were the ones responsible for controlling some of the moods that we experienced.

Happiness, for instance, was an emotion that came from the heart, while anger is an emotion that stemmed from the liver. Fear, another primary emotion, was produced by the kidneys.

Charles Darwin, on the other hand, believed that emotions were useful to us, particularly for evolutionary purposes.
Darwin believed that it was our emotions which greatly enhanced the chances of the human species' survival.

The brain relied on emotions to warn us when danger was present and keep us away from it by generating fear.

It also, according to Darwin, protected our health by generating disgust, which stopped us from consuming spoiled food, helped us maintain control over our resources through anger, and encouraged us to feel good by pursuing the things that made us happy.

Very interesting indeed.

Facts You Might Not Know About Emotions

The biggest motivator behind the actions that we take is emotions.

We love, we survive, we behave morally, and we create social bonds and more, all because we are spurred by the emotions that flow through our beings.
These chemicals which flow through us are a direct response to the way we view and perceive what is happening in the world around us.

Plutchick got it right when he identified that there were 8 types of basic human emotions that were experienced universally, but there's more to emotions than just the 8 alone.

As it turns out, emotions are more interesting than we thought, and these interesting facts might just be what we need to help us better understand why we feel and react the way that we do:

- **Fact: They Are the Key to Our Survival**
  We wouldn't have lasted as long as we did without them.

When the early humans had to hunt to survive, they relied on their emotions to keep them alive and stay one step ahead of their prey.

Fear kept them alert and motivated to take a specific action, warning them to stay vigilant so they didn't end up becoming the prey.

In today's society, happiness keeps us motivated to keep working towards our goals.

Frustration pushes us to find a solution to our problems. Every emotion has a meaning and a specific purpose and understanding the reasons *behind these emotions* will help us better understand them.

When we can understand what we seek to control, that's when we learn to become the master.

- **Fact: They Are Neutral**

Not all, but some of them are.

Some emotions are neither good nor bad. We tend to think of emotions as being either one extreme or the other, but that might not necessarily be the right approach to take.

Take happiness and sadness for example. It seems obvious at first glance that the former is a positive (good) emotion, while the latter is bad (negative).

Yet, these two emotions might have more in common than it seems. You feel happy when you get what you want, and you feel sad when you don't get what you want.
These emotions, therefore, are two sides of a similar need, and one can't exist without the other.

Every emotion serves a purpose, even the difficult ones, and they all work to balance each other out somehow.

- **Fact: They're Contagious**

This one is probably obvious. Emotions can infect in an instant.

When you're around someone who is brimming with happiness, it's hard not to smile and feel a positive burst of energy yourself because their happiness is radiating unto you.

Both positive and negative emotions can be infectious, and just like how you're able to feel happy off someone else's happiness, you can easily be just as affected if their mood was on the negative side too.

This goes back to the evolutionary aspect of being human, in the days when we as a species thrived and survived by living together in groups.

Because of this, the early humans had to depend on one another to survive, and one of the ways they did that was to rely on someone else's emotions.

If they saw fear in someone, they're likely to respond much quicker and be alert to the danger that was present.

Seeing the fear in another activated their own fear response simultaneously, and this spurred them to take the action they needed to survive.
Despite what introverts might claim, it is built within us to be social creatures.

We crave the company of others and feel miserable when we feel lonely and isolated from the rest of the world.

Today, we continue to pick on each other's emotions, even that of strangers. When we see someone crying, we know that something is wrong and we reach out to give them the help they need.

This form of nonverbal communication is one of the most unique things that make us human, and bonds all of us together, even if we may be strangers.

- **Fact: They Are Not the Same as Feelings**
They're not the same as moods either. Although we do say *"I feel...."* to try and explain the emotion that we're experiencing, emotions and feelings are two very different concepts.

Interrelated, yes. But different.

Emotions take time to happen because they rely on the chemicals produced in response to certain triggers, and it takes about ¼ seconds before our brains can correctly identify first the trigger, and then another ¼ second to produce the necessary chemicals which result in emotions.

Feelings, on the other hand, are the product of what happens when we start to *think* about these emotions and let it sink in. They last much longer than emotions do, and they can sometimes be fueled by a combination of several feelings at once.

Our moods, on the other hand, can be influenced heavily by several factors which include our environment, our physiology, and our mental state. Our moods, depending on what they are, could last any amount of time. Minutes, hours, days, maybe even weeks.

- **Fact: Your Emotions Are Always Obvious on Your Face**

The expression *"It's written all over your face"* literally means exactly that when it comes to your emotions.

Verbally, you may say that you're fine, but your body language—in this case, your facial expression - will always give you away. Even when you try to conceal how you really feel, we still emit what is known as micro expressions, which are brief, fleeting emotions that tend to come out involuntarily.

These micro expressions happen quickly, sometimes happening so fast it's hard to see with the naked eye. But when these expressions are recorded and they played back again in slow motion, they can reveal a fascinating story behind what a person is truly feeling.

- **Fact: Bad Emotions Can Sometimes Be Good**
This might sound like the opposite of what's been discussed so far, but what we need to remember is that life is about balance.

There must be some negative emotions to balance out the good ones.

Although we might want to feel positive and happy all the time, that's not exactly healthy either, since it might lead to ignoring serious issues which need to be addressed simply because we don't want to face reality.

- **Fact: Emotions Allow for Expression**
Despite what some people might think, emotions are not a sign that you're weak. Emotions are a form of expression, the way that we let other people know what we're going through.

Again, emotions matter and this time they serve as important insight and clues into what you're going through and what the next step that you might have to take is.

We need to listen to our emotions at times and determine if they're trying to tell us something.

The next time you feel a particularly strong emotion, try *listening* to what it's telling you instead of suppressing or dismissing it altogether.

- **Fact: Sleep Helps**

   Getting enough sleep helps with your emotions. Whenever you're feeling distressed, it could be aggravated even further if you're lacking sleep. During the REM (Rapid Eye Movement) stage of our sleep cycle is when the stress-related hormones we produced are reduced significantly.

   It is during this stage that our brains start to mellow down, and lessen the pain that we feel from the emotions that caused us distressed in the first place since the chemicals responsible for these emotions are not being produced while we sleep.

   If you're feeling particularly emotional, try to get enough sleep and notice what a difference it makes in the way that you think and feels when you wake up the next morning.

- **Fact: Emotions Help Define Your Morals**

  Which comes first? Emotions or morals? Believe it or not, it's our *emotions* that actually come first, and they're responsible for shaping our morals.

  A study was conducted into this subject; the findings revealed that when the participant(s) involved were shown images of a person being hurt by another, three distinctive parts of the brain were lit up.

  First was the brain's TPJ area, which was responsible for determining if that person was being hurt intentionally.

  The second part of the brain to light up was the amygdala, which is the part that controls our emotions.

  It was only *after* those two phases did the morality portion of the brain start to kick in. So yes, it is, in fact, our *emotions that shape our morals.*

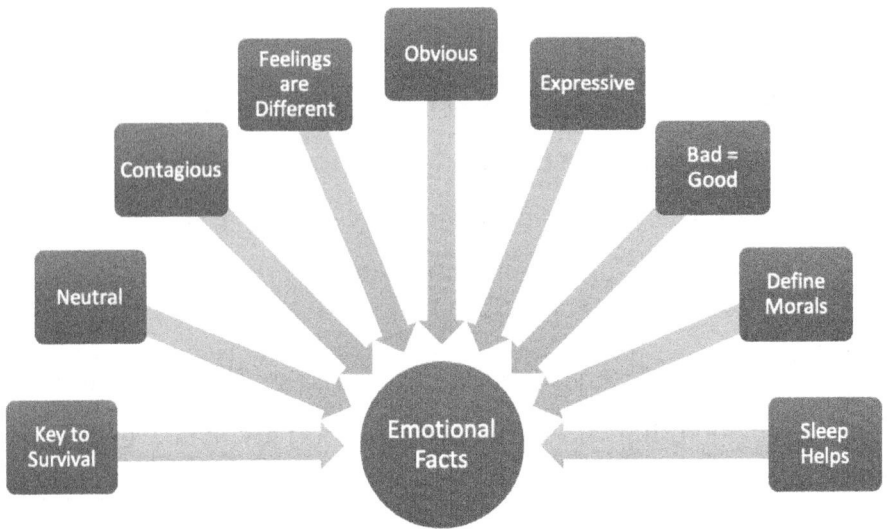

Facts about Emotions

You have to right to feel every emotion that you experience, and don't let anyone tell you otherwise.

Each of us is entitled to our own feelings, and they are a part of who we are. It is never wrong to be feeling the way that you do, and it is a myth to believe that it is wrong to feel emotional.

From what we now understand so far about emotions, they have served us well and helped us survive for as long as we have, and they will continue to help us survive for years to come.

Your emotions are not wrong, but the way that you handle and regulate them could probably be better.

The truth is, everyone is capable of better managing their emotions. They just need the right coping mechanism and techniques to do it.

How Mentally Strong People Control Their Emotions

There is a reason mentally strong people are more successful at controlling their emotions and regulating them in an almost effortless manner (or so it seems).

It's because they are practicing certain habits which you are not.

They have found and developed techniques and habits of regulating their emotions which work for them, they have trained themselves to have the needed discipline to stick to those habits. They have made it a part of their lifestyle to a point that managing their emotions now becomes second nature to them. This is what you're aspiring to accomplish right now.

Your mind is the most powerful asset you possess. It can either make you, or it can break you.

Why some people find it difficult to make even the simplest of goals a reality while others are pushing boundaries and redefining their future is
because negativity is something your mind constantly has to contend with.

The problem with negativity is how much of an influence it has, how much power it wields.
It's the reason your emotions are going to overpower you, even more, when you're too wired up to think logically and with reason.

- **They Don't Give Up**
  Oh, the temptation to do it is definitely there. But they don't give into it.

  That's what makes them so tough in the first place.
  When the going gets tough, it can be tempting to give in to the desire to quit, admit defeat and run away.

  But those are exactly the instincts you need to battle against. The minute you do, your hope of being tougher mentally diminishes just a little bit more with each defeat.

You are capable of so much more than you give yourself credit for.

You have overcome difficult situations in the past, you need to now make it a habit of doing it all the time.

> "Never give up, for that is just the place and time that the tide will turn."
>
> — Harriet Beecher Stowe

- **They're Focused**

    Mentally tough people have trained themselves to have intense focus.

    They can be so focused on a goal that they refused to back down or give up until the goal has been accomplished.

To master this habit, you would need to become a master of self-discipline.

You don't have to restrict yourself and your lifestyle to a point that you're unhappy and wondering why you did this, it's about striking a balance, knowing when you should resist temptation and controlling the urge to always give in to your desires.

Like when your emotions may urge you to fly off the handle, even when you know that you shouldn't.

> "Successful people maintain a positive focus in life no matter what is going on around them."
>
> — Jack Canfield

- **They Give Themselves a Purpose**
  A mentally tough person gets out of bed each morning with a purpose.

They tell themselves *"Today, I will not let my emotions get the best of me"* and they commit to seeing it through.

They train themselves to wake up each day with a purpose and the intention to get things done is what helps keep them on track to keeping their emotions in check.

> "He who has a why to live for can bear almost any how."
>
> — Friedrich Nietzsche

- **They Have a System That Works for Them**

  The reason you find it difficult to maintain control over your emotions is that the current system which you have is probably not working well for you.

If that is the case, then it's time to copy what the mentally strong people do and create your own system which works for you.

If it helps you to physically walk away from the situation and take a few minutes to compose yourself, do it and don't apologize for it.

This is your coping system that works, and if this is what you need to get you one step closer to mastering your emotions, do it.

- **They're Willing to Put in The Work for It**
What a lot of people fail to realize is that learning to control your emotions is not something that can be done overnight.

It's a skill that you need to work for and work hard. Emotionally intelligent and mentally strong people are not born with it, it's not a talent that they automatically possess.

They are mentally strong and seem to have self-discipline by the bucket load because they work hard at maintaining it.

They know they want it, they know why they need it, they put in the work to develop it, and they work hard at keeping it every single day.

> "Successful people are not gifted, they just work hard, then succeed on purpose."
>
> — G.K. Nelson

- **They *KNOW* It's Worth the Hard Work**

  Mentally strong people know that it's not easy, but they know the hard work that they put it is going to be worth it.

  A lot of the times when we set goals or targets for ourselves, the end result won't materialize immediately.

When we don't see that happening, we begin to lose that luster and that zest we started out with.
We begin to wonder if all this extra effort is worth it.

Mentally tough people go through this same process too, but the difference is, they *know it's worth* the hard work that they put it.

It is much easier for you to just say this isn't for you and give up, but it would be a real shame to quit before you've even had a chance to see it through.

That's something mentally strong people would never do.

> "The successful warrior is the average man, with laser-like focus."
>
> — Bruce Lee

- **They Surround Themselves with Positivity**

Misery loves company, and you can bet if you surround yourself with toxic, negative individuals that you're going to be sucked into that vortex of unhappiness too.

Are you surrounded by the right company? Are they highly emotional people?

We may not give much thought to the company that we keep, but too much negativity can subconsciously influence us more than we realize.

Not having enough positivity in your life is not going to make it any easier for you to attempt to master your emotions since it's harder to think with a clear head when you're caught up in your own unhappiness.

> "Surround yourself with people that reflect who you want to be and how you want to feel."
>
> — Rachel Wolchin

- **They Don't Focus on The Past**

  One thing that all mentally strong individuals do is that they never allow the past to hold them back.

  Sure, things may not have worked out before, and there might have been several emotional mishaps that they wish they could take back. Sure, they may have failed once, twice, or maybe several times over.

  But the difference is, they don't use those reasons as an excuse to hold themselves back.

  If you continue using your past failures and letting that be the reason you're afraid because you think you might fail again if you tried, then you'll always have excuses not to make the necessary changes that you need for the better.

  Learning to control your emotions may not be easy, and you might stumble several times along the way, but if you don't try, you'll never know.

> "The past cannot be changed. The future is yet in your power."
>
> — Unknown

- **They Are Willing to Be Flexible**

Nothing can cause a sudden stir of frustrating emotions than when things do not go your way.

When you think you've thought out and planned your action steps so meticulously and still fail, that disappointment is not always an easy emotion to contend with.

The first step towards controlling your thoughts the way mentally tough people do and not letting it get the best of you is to accept that nothing is ever fully in your control.

As long as you had done your very best, that's all you can ask for.

Your best has to be good enough and when it isn't, be flexible enough and willing to adapt and make the necessary changes needed to bounce back on track.

That's what a mentally strong person would do.

> "Most of the important things in the world have been accomplished by people who have kept on trying when there seemed to be no help at all."
>
> — Dale Carnegie

- **They Don't Give in To Worry**

    There's always going to be a reason to worry that you might lose control of your emotions at any time, but why worry about what you cannot change?

    Mentally tough people don't do that. They know that worrying does nothing except waste your precious time, which could instead be spent devising strategies to help you get to the next phase of your mission to master your emotions.

Successful people are mentally tough because they do not waste their energy on what is beyond their control.

Instead, they shift their focus toward what needs to be done. If it works it works, if it doesn't they find a way to make it work the next time they attempt it.

Being a habitual worrier will only sow seeds of doubt in your mind, and that is not something you need if you want to build a tougher mind.

> "If you are not willing to risk the usual you will have to settle for the ordinary."
>
> — Jim Rohn

- **They're Not Afraid of Pushing Their Boundaries**

Nothing will propel you faster towards a tougher frame of mind than by consistently challenging yourself at every opportunity.

Mentally strong people train themselves to be that way, and one approach to doing it is to pick something that they find challenging and make it a goal to overcome it.

It doesn't have to be anything major, as long as it pushed their boundaries.

Here's a simple example of an exercise in pushing your boundaries that you could do.

If you have never run a mile before—so that the next time you're out for a run. Don't stop until you have achieved that target, even if you feel like your legs are about to give up and you want badly to quit.

When you make it, congratulate yourself. The time after, make it a mile and a half.

Then add another, and another, *and another again* with each run session you take on.

That's one way of pushing your boundaries, and the training comes from not wanting to quit even when you want to.

> "There will be obstacles. There will be doubters. There will be mistakes. But with hard work, there are no limits."
>
> — Michael Phelps

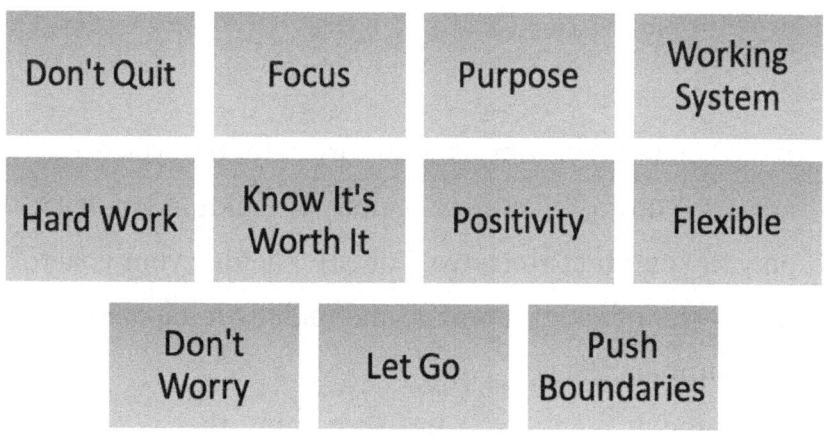

Traits of Mentally Strong Individuals

Learning to develop a tougher mindset is going to benefit you in a lot of ways. For one thing, it is going to improve your confidence, which is crucial if you want to overcome the obstacles you are going to encounter along the way towards mastering your emotions.

Mental toughness is going to make you more resilient because having a tough mindset means you have determination, grit, and willpower to a point that you will not be deterred by anything that is going to attempt to stop you.

You will take each challenge in stride, which is something that can only happen over time, and it begins by cultivating a tough frame of mind.

Being mentally strong is going to empower you to keep going because you feel like there is nothing holding you back, and the only thought that you have is about reaching your goal to become the master of your emotions, and making it happen is going to be your primary focus.

Being tough mentally is not something that is out of reach. If others could learn how to do it, you can too. You too can learn to control your emotions and shape your mindset to become what *you want it to be.*

Repercussions of Ignoring or Suppressing Your Emotions

You know how to deal with emotions. You just sometimes choose *not to* because they can be unpleasant.

Nobody likes facing their negative emotions, Anxiety, disappointment, jealousy, anger, rage, depression.

They're all unpleasant, and it's our instinct to try and avoid or stay away from anything that doesn't feel good.

So, when you start to feel negative emotions creeping in, you do your best to ignore them by shutting them out, suppressing them, and denying them.
You try to run away from them and hope that they'll go away on their own.

That's what most people do, and that's what we've all been taught since we were old enough to understand the consequences of having certain emotions.

Be strong. Don't cry. Toughen up. Don't make a big deal out of it. Talking about it makes it worse. Crying doesn't help. Just be positive. You're overreacting.

These are the common phrases we've been accustomed to hearing all our life.
You've spent most of your life bottling things up, keeping it to yourself and trying your best to put a smile on your face, hoping that things will "just get better".

Rarely are we ever encouraged to face our emotions head on that when they start to overwhelm us, we don't know what to do with them.

By suppressing your emotions, you're trapping yourself in a mental prison, and that's where you'll continue to stay until you open that door and let yourself out.

You've been told all your life to suppress your emotions and put on a brave face because other people *don't know how to deal* with emotions either.

Even you might not know what to do when you see someone crying or having an emotional moment in front of you, except to feel uncomfortable and wish you were anywhere else but here.

If there's one thing about emotions you need to always remember, it is this.

Suppressing them is never a good idea, and it never works. Ever. By ignoring your emotions, you're doing more harm than good. Researchers have already done a study into the subject of suppressing your emotions and the impact that it has on sleep quality, and what they discovered is what we've known deep down all along.

The participants involved in the study who kept their emotions buried inside experience more anxiety, sadness, anger and fear in their dreams than those who didn't.

They also had more difficulty sleeping and struggled with tiredness during the day. When they did sleep, their sleep was often interrupted. In their everyday lives, these participants also experienced more stress, unhappiness, anxiety, and depression than the participants who expressed their emotions regularly.

Here are some other things that get compromised when you choose to deny your emotions:

- **You Burn Out from Being "Busy"**

    You're not technically "busy", you're finding extra ways to occupy your time, so you don't have a quiet moment to yourself.

    Because in these quiet moments, you might be forced to face your emotions, and rather than deal with them, you trying to keep yourself as occupied as possible.

    While it is good to remain productive, we're not built to keep working to such extremes, and you put yourself at risk of burning out when you pack on one task after another. All because you would rather avoid dealing with your emotions.

- **You Start Caring Too Much About Others**

While this may sound like a good thing (and in some cases it is), if it's costing you your own emotional and mental wellbeing, it becomes a problem.

When you're always prioritizing the needs of others before your own, it becomes a problem.

When you choose to ignore your emotions to make others happy, it's a problem.

You matter just as much as everyone else does, and your wellbeing should never be compromised.

It may feel easier to try and help someone work through their emotions instead of dealing with your own, but it always results in you feeling more tired, drained and even unhappier than you initially were.

- **You Become Isolated**
When you're not feeling great, you lack the desire to socialize and be around others.

You don't feel like going out, you put off responding to texts and emails, and you put up invisible walls you don't even realize when you disengage from the rest of the world.

You become just as shut in as your emotions are, and that is never a good thing when relationships start to become compromised.

- **You Become a Different Person**
Hurting on the inside has a way of changing you.

When you're in pain and not dealing with it, you're pretending to be someone that you're not. You put a smile on your face, even though you feel like crying on the inside. You try to pretend everything is okay when it's not. You become withdrawn, and eventually closed-off because you feel like nobody understands you.

It hurts to feel like no one cares enough to help you, but how can they when they don't understand what you're going through?

- **Newer Anxieties Develop**

Repressed emotions are like water boiling in the kettle. Sooner or later, it's going to come to a boil and the whistle is going to blow, signaling that it has reached its limit.

When these emotions start to boil and reach its limit, that's when we come close to our breaking point. That's when emotional outbursts happen.

Alternatively, instead of an emotional outburst, what might happen instead is that your emotions start to find other avenues of manifesting themselves.

One way is by creating new anxieties which might not have existed in the past.

Maybe it's become harder for you to socialize, maybe you're now anxious about leaving the house because it has become such a draining ordeal.

Suppressed emotions will never stay bottled in for long, they'll always find a way to come out. Always.

- **You Become a Control Freak**

The feeling of losing control over emotions might cause some people to compensate by seeking control in other aspects of their lives.

You try to control every other aspect of your life (except your emotions) and become increasingly frustrated or angry when things don't go your way.

You try to plan and map out as much detail of your day as possible, at work and in your personal life, and when things don't go according to plan, it feels like your emotions are about to burst through the surface again and the internal battle continues to try and keep it in.

Despite knowing that some things are beyond your control, that still doesn't stop you from feeling unhappy when you fail to control the situation.

- **It Becomes Impossible to Heal and Forgive**
People will hurt you along the way, that's the way things are.

There's no one alive who can tell you that they have never been hurt by another. As long as you're around people, there's always a chance of getting hurt.

Suppressing your emotions, on the other hand, makes it harder for you to heal from that hurt and learn to forgive.

When you get stuck holding onto the hurt, you're trapping yourself in the past, and that will always hold you back from making any genuine relationships in the future.

You'll always think about how you've been hurt, which will compromise your ability to trust.

Learning to heal, move on and forgive is not possible when you don't want to confront those emotions inside you.

You need to stop ignoring what comes naturally to you. Emotions are who we are, and denying them would be like denying we had arms or legs.

As long as you're alive, you will *always* feel a range of emotions throughout your lifetime, and it's better to learn how to master them rather than suppress them.

Chapter 4: Doing Away with Negativity

If there's one group of emotions we should do away with, it's negativity.

Being plagued with negative emotions weighing on your mind only makes it that much harder to overcome your challenges.

It does beyond just "feeling sad" or "feeling unhappy". Negativity is an actual hindrance, stopping your brain from performing the clear-thinking process that it needs to deal with complex tasks.

When we can't think clearly enough to process the information on hand, it's easier for issues to seem bigger than what they are.
Add stress into the mix, and perhaps a dash of anger and it quite literally seems impossible to function normally when all your mind can focus on is how your emotions seem to be getting out of control with each passing minute.

Initiating change has to begin with you.

Tell yourself that you have no time for excuses anymore, the only action that is going to yield results.

Excuses only serve as barriers towards accomplishing your goals, and there is no room for that in your life.

Say yes when you feel like saying no, and tell yourself you can do it even if it feels impossible.
You *can* overcome negativity. You *can* overcome anxiety. You *can* minimize your stress, anger, and anxiety. You can do anything you set your mind to, including mastering your emotions eventually.

Your mind is the very foundation of everything that you do. Your mindset affects your decisions, your thoughts, the actions and choices you make.

Changing your mindset is simply training your mind to see the world around you in a different light, and mindset matters because the way you view yourself and the world around you shapes the reality that you live in.

How to Overcome Negativity

Mental preparation is the key to overcoming negativity.

Some of the most successful people in the world start their day every morning by mentally preparing themselves for the day ahead.

They meditate, use positive affirmations, recite their goals to themselves or even listen to motivational podcasts on their phones or other mobile devices.

Essentially, they do whatever it takes to prepare their mind to focus on blocking out and minimize the impact of any kind of negativity they are going to encounter.

Life is going to put you through a myriad of emotions. You're going to experience everything from fear, excitement, stress, pressure, passion, determination and more.

There is one thing that is going to help you get through it all and come out triumphant on the other side—overcoming negativity.

- **Think About It**
  When a negative thought pops into our heads, we don't stop to think enough if this is a thought that should be taken seriously.

  Is there really a cause for alarm? Or could be perhaps be exaggerating the thought in our minds, making it sound worse than what it really is.

  Some negative thoughts and emotions are triggered by external factors.

  You might be tired, hungry, exhausted, overworked or already feeling tense at the time of the negative thought, and it probably aggravated the situation.

  When you're already not in the best frame of mind, a small issue can seem worse than what it is.

The next time you find yourself dwelling on a negative thought, stop and think about it for a minute and ask yourself if it's justified.

- **Have an Action Plan**

    There are always going to be challenges which are unpleasant. We can't run away from it, even if we wanted to.

    But viewing those challenges from a negative perspective is only going to make things much worse for you.

    Having a plan of action on the other hand about what you can do to manage the unexpected un-pleasantries that life may occasionally throw your way will keep you moving forward and no longer be held back despite the negativity that you feel.

    When Plan A fails, have a Plan B, a Plan C, and as many back-up plans as you need.

    Be as adaptable and fluid as water, ever ready to twist and turn to continue forging a path forward, because that's the only way to go forward.

Having a plan as opposed to having no plan at all, helps you manage the way you feel.

- **Think About What's Helpful**

  Whenever you've experienced a setback, the last thing you might be thinking about is how this situation is helpful to you.

  As bleak or negative as a situation may be, one trick mentally tough individuals use to help them maintain their optimism is to think about what helpful lesson they can take away from the setbacks they experienced.

  It could be one lesson, it could be two, it could be as many lessons as you'd like.

  No matter how bad things seem, there's always a silver lining, it's up to you to find it by asking yourself the right questions.

  Questions like *what have I learned from this experience? What can I do to make it better moving forward? What's one positive takeaway from this situation?*
- **Observe Your Surroundings**

Your environment has a big impact on the way that you feel. The place you spend most of your time is going to weigh on your mind subconsciously. You may not be actively thinking about your surroundings, but it's there in the back of your mind.

If you find it hard to remain positive throughout the day, do a quick scan of your surroundings and observe what the sources of negativity may be.

Your cluttered workstation? The toxic colleague who is constantly complaining and talking negatively about other colleagues behind their back?

Maybe that pile of paperwork you've been postponing for a while now and haven't gotten around to doing yet.

Once you've identified a potential source, ask yourself what you can do to rectify the problem.

Can the source be removed entirely? If it can't what else could you do to spend less time around this negative source in a week?

- **Stop Feeding into Your Thoughts**

Feeding into your negative thoughts is only going to fuel it to become even more out of control.

A thought may start off small, but the more you continue to obsess and dwell over the matter, the bigger that thought eventually seems to become.

The expression *making a mountain out of a molehill* is completely applicable to this situation.

We sometimes build up our fears so much in our minds that they seem disastrous until we eventually face them and come to realize it wasn't so bad after all.

- **Find Inspiration Daily**

The best way to cultivate a positive mindset and minimize negativity is to wake up each morning and make the first thing that you see something that is going to inspire you.

Pick a quote or a saying, stick pictures of inspirational quotes on your mirrors, in your cubicle at work, a note on your phone, make it your wallpaper on your computer, and just surround yourself with it so it's hard to miss.

Starting off on a positive note will help set the tone for the rest of the day, so wake up each morning and let positivity be the first and dominant feeling that helps to start your day right.

Every day is another chance, another opportunity to begin anew, and it is what you do today - *not what has happened in the past* - that matters most.

- **Cultivate Positive Dialogue**

    We've established by now just how powerful your thoughts can be. If your thoughts have the power to influence negativity, they also have that same power to do the opposite.

    You need to start tapping into that force and begin creating a more optimistic mindset.

    You must push every negative thought you have about yourself out of your mind and start replacing it with something positive instead.

    Imagine your negative thoughts as physical boulders in front of you, and you need to forcefully push those out of your mind and clear the path for newer, better things.

For every negative thought that you find yourself thinking, stop and immediately replace that thought with a positive one.

- **Reshape Your Failure Perspective**
Instead of thinking about them as failures, see them as lessons instead.

They're not failures, they're learning experiences that teach you what *not to do*, and what needs improvement.

We are constantly learning something new, always growing and developing into a better version of yourself. Nobody can do everything perfectly, or always get it from the first go without taking a few stumbles along the way.

Every successful person out there today that has made their mark and becomes a household name didn't get to where they are without taking a few tumbles and stumbles along the way.

They too made plenty of mistakes before they got to the pinnacle of success.

Change your mind set by changing the way you see these failures, don't focus on how you failed but instead, start thinking about how you can improve next time or what you can do differently.

- **Keep Your Company Positive**

    Negative people will only weigh you down. They'll drain you of energy, become a mental and emotional burden that you don't need.

    When you surround yourself with people who think positive, you'll slowly adapt the way you think to emulate them as their wisdom, their outlook, stories, and affirmations slowly seep into your own way of thinking.

    Examine the people in your life right now, and if there are any individuals in it who are toxic with their negative outlook, it's time to start distancing yourself from them.

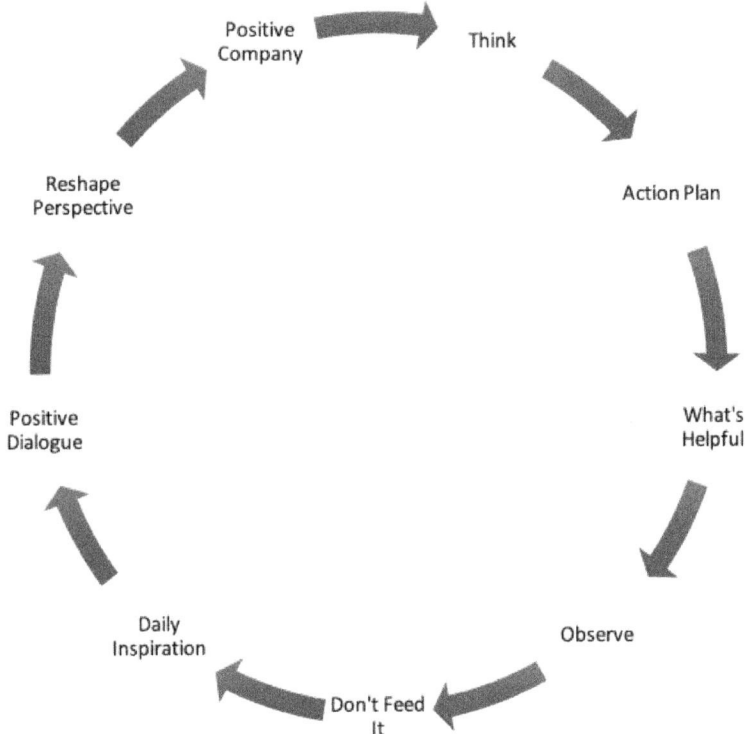

How to Overcome Negative Thoughts

You need to believe in yourself. Believe that you are stronger than you give yourself credit for, believe that you deserve to have a better, happier life.

You'll never truly achieve the level of positive mindset you hope for if you still have those nagging thoughts at the back of your mind that make you doubt yourself every step of the way.

Whenever you feel your emotions getting the better of you, stop and take a breath.

Focusing on your breathing will help you shift your focus and your mind from feeling anxious, nervous, scared or angry to calm, steadiness and peace.

By believing you can achieve it, you've already put yourself one step closer to making it happen for real.

How to Reduce Anxiety

Anxiety is one of the things that could happen to you. You didn't ask for it.

Nobody would ever choose to feel tense and anxious over being happy and comfortable.

Those who tend to worry chronically are always surrounded by an impending sense of doom, or unrealistic fears that tend to magnify and increase their worries.

There's no one who would ever voluntarily want to put themselves in this position.

Anxiety just happen due to a number of factors and having them doesn't make you weak.

Anxiety is mainly caused by worry, and worry could stem from several factors.

For example, we worry that we might lose control of our emotions and react in a way we'll regret when it's done.

When we lose that sense of control, that's when we start to worry and obsess.
Not being able to fully control the situation goes against the very nature of some people who need to have that control to feel secure.

Because of that, they have a hard time coping and start worrying and thinking about the possible ways things could go wrong.

Eventually, this leads to anxiety.

Another possible cause for worry is our jobs. Job security is not a luxury that everyone can afford, and it is natural to worry on some level that we may be out of a job at any time.

Even if we lose our jobs, the bills still need to be paid because they never stop coming, and we worry about how we are going to do that with no income.

Anxiety over losing your job overwhelm you to a point where it starts to affect your productivity. Understandably, the stress of being made redundant is very real, and when combined with the external pressures such as the competitive job market, the worries seem endless and anxiety naturally follows suit.

Worry could be caused by several factors, each one as valid as the next.

Never dismiss your emotions and the way you feel, you have every right to experience the emotions that you do.

Am I Experience Anxiety? Or Just Worry?

We all worry from time to time.

There will be moments in life that make you more anxious than others. Moments where you might feel intense bouts of worry. But when does normal worry stop being normal and cross over into anxiety?

There is a fine line between worry and anxiety, and these are the signs to look out for that sets anxiety apart:

- **Your Fears Are Crippling You**
  Being afraid of something is one thing, being so crippled by that fear that you're unable to think or react rationally – or sometimes not being able to react at all – is anxiety.

  Some fears can be so crippling that they morph into full-on panic attacks.

  These are no fun to deal with.

  If you're experiencing a sense of helplessness, along with being so gripped by fear that it starts to manifest itself physically causing you to sweat, feel weak, dizzy, nauseous, and even have difficulty breathing—what you've got on your hands is most definitely a sign of anxiety.

- **You Have Difficulty Falling Asleep at Night**
  Do you lie awake in bed at night, worrying? Stressed, perhaps? Agitated or nervous? Try as you might fall asleep, it simply isn't working?

Insomnia or trouble falling asleep because you can't stop worrying is a sign that what you're dealing with is anxiety.

- **Your Life Revolves Around Your Worry**
  Worrying about things every now and again is normal, but when that worry happens more than it should and is accompanied by other symptoms such as an inability to focus because your mind is too busy worrying, fatigue and headaches, that's when your worry is no longer a worry, but now a form of anxiety.

Persistent worrying or anxious thoughts that never seem to go away and plague you nearly every moment of your waking hours is one way you know that you're dealing with anxiety.

- **You Have Trouble Focusing**
  Anxious thoughts have a way of consuming you as they slowly start to take over.

Difficulty concentrating on even the simplest of tasks because your mind either goes blank or starts to worry again is another sign that you're dealing with anxiety.

This is a sure sign you've got to do something about it since the inability to concentrate is going to affect your performance at work and productivity levels.

- **You're Always Tense**

    You can't even remember the last time you felt relaxed. Your muscles are always sore from the invisible tension you're carrying around.

    Anxiety will do that to you, it's one way that it manifests itself physically, in the form of soreness and muscular aches.

Overcoming Anxiety

Struggling with anxiety is not easy. Those who do can be affected so much by their reasons to be anxious and are so overcome with worry that it starts to interfere with their daily routine.

Anxiety, when experienced at more severe levels, could even hamper them from functioning normally. Even the smallest of tasks like getting out of bed can suddenly prove to be too much, because anxiety is crippling, and anything suddenly becomes a possible threat.

Anxiety is not something that should be taken lightly, because there have been instances where chronic worriers are so anxiety-ridden that they start to become involved in harmful habits such as turning to alcohol, drugs, smoking and sometimes even overeating in a false attempt to make themselves feel better.

In worst case scenarios, their levels of anxiety and worry can be so high that it can lead to depressive and even suicidal thoughts.

With the right strategies and the right techniques, we are all capable of overcoming our anxieties. Imagine yourself as an athlete, a runner perhaps, and your anxiety is the hurdle that has been placed in front of you. Imagine how incredible it would feel once you leap over that hurdle and reached the other side. Anxieties can be minimized and overcome with patience and the right practical strategies.

Constantly being plagued by persistently negative, worrying thoughts can make it difficult for anyone to concentrate. The good news is, there are several strategies that can be used to help you beat your anxiety, and if one doesn't work as well for you, there are plenty of others for you to choose from. There's a right strategy for everyone.

Most of the time, the fears that stem from anxiety have no real basis, no foundation and no firm foothold to stand on.

For every negative thought that is caused by anxiety, there is something that can be done to overcome it. One such approach to take is through positive affirmations.

The mind is a very powerful thing, and we can easily become a prisoner of our own thoughts without even realizing that it is happening until it is too late.

But that means that our minds are just as capable, just as strong enough to turn things around if we wanted it to, and the strongest tool at your disposal to start training your mind is through these positive affirmations.

The affirmations can be used to replace the negative thoughts that dwell within your mind causing you to feel anxious. Part of challenging yourself to change and to gradually rebuild your self-confidence is to simply follow the same method that happens when you have a negative thought stemming from anxiety.

Instead of allowing those negative thoughts to overcome your mind, use a positive affirmation as a thought replacement instead.

Come up with your own little list of positive affirmations, sayings that make you feel good about yourself each time that you say it.

Each time you feel your anxiety rising, fall back on your list positive affirmations and start repeating them until it sinks in and you start to feel your mind calming down.

Here are some examples of positive affirmations you could include in your list to help you get started:

- I am more than capable of remaining calm and collected.
- I am stronger than my anxieties.
- I love myself unconditionally.
- I am confident enough to overcome all my problems.
- I believe in myself.
- I believe in myself in everything that I do
- I can overcome anything when I put my mind to it.
- Anxiety has no power over me.
- I am strong and challenges only make me stronger.
- I am in control of my thoughts and I choose to be positive.
- Anxiety does not control me, and it never will.
- I am getting better every single day, and I am getting stronger.

- I am grateful for everything I have in my life.

Affirmations can be as positive and effective as you want them to be.

They can be anything you want them to be too.

Choose your own phrases, words, and sentences that make you feel empowered and strong.

To see success with these affirmations, you need to make a dedicated effort towards practicing it consistently.

Forcing yourself to believe in them is not going to work, these affirmations will take time to sink in because they need to gradually build momentum and strength with time to finally overpower your anxious thoughts.

It may prove to be a bit of a struggle, but eventually, it will get easier as it goes on.

Affirmations are the key to changing your perspective, but it's not going to happen overnight. No, this needs to be a part of your daily routine if you want to experience real change in your life and eventual freedom from the crippling fear that anxiety brings.

Create a habit of repeating your positive affirmations to yourself every morning.

Train your mind to get used to hearing this positive dialogue repeated every day, and thus, your mind will gradually shift towards this more positive outlook without you even realizing it.

You begin feeling better about yourself after a while once these positive affirmations have become a habit. As your mind shifts out of the negative shroud of anxiety, you will gradually begin to regain your confidence again.

A large part of the prevention of anxiety is having awareness about what is causing it. Identifying your triggers, in particular. Learning to identify your anxious thoughts when they come up can help you control and reduce them quickly.

If you're not sure whether your anxiety is triggered by a medical condition, or a byproduct of bad experiences, treating anxiety early is always easier than when it gets worse over time.

To be on the safe side, you should consider getting the opinion of an expert or doctor if:

- Your anxiety is affecting you enough that you can't function normally in your routine. This includes your work, school or social life.
- You feel the need to use substances such as alcohol or drugs to manage your anxiety.
- Your fear or worry feels like it's out of your control.
- You are having suicidal thoughts
- You have the tendency to self-harm.
- You strongly feel that your anxiety is caused by a serious mental health condition.

How to Minimize Stress, Anger, and Worry

All of us have just one life to live. *One*. That's all we get, and that makes each moment precious.

Once a moment has passed you by, it's gone forever. You can never get it back again.

Life has a lot to offer, despite its ups and downs, and every minute that is spent worrying, stressing and being angry is a moment that is wasted.

You're missing out on the present, which is often the best part of life.

Anger, worry and stress are three of the least constructive emotions to spend your time on.

Fretting and predicting the possible problems of the future is not productive, generating solutions to fix those problems or prevent them, is construction.

Problem-solving is good, worrying is not. If you've spent far too much of your life worrying about the unnecessary, isn't it time to change that pattern of behavior?

Worrying distracts you from the more important things in life, and the things that you should be doing.

Those who worry fall into a cycle of obsessing and dwelling about the possible negative things which are either happening to them or possibly going to happen in the future.

They are too preoccupied with their worries, they eventually end up neglecting the things that matter. When you worry or feel anxious all the time, it becomes hard for you to make decisions.

Each decision seems like it would come with its own set of problems and possible negative outcomes, which causes you to worry even more.

When you finally do decide, it may not necessarily be the right decision because your judgment has been clouded by worry.

When chronic worrying becomes a habit, you lose your ability to see the silver lining in any situation. All you can think about and focus on are the negatives.

Losing the ability to see the positive side of situations will increase your levels of anxiety and fear and do nothing to help quell the overwhelming sense of worry that you feel.

Eventually, it becomes almost impossible to view things positively, even when there is nothing bad to think about.
For all of these reasons and more, you need to start working on minimizing the stress, anger and worry that you feel, and this is how you do it:

You're also going to need some practical, easy to follow methods to help you cope with anxiety, anger, and worry to keep it under control.

You may not be able to get rid of it entirely, but at least it will help provide some relief when you don't feel like you're losing control of your emotions all the time:

- **Confide in Those You Can Trust**
  It makes a world of difference when you know you've got one, two or several people that you can count on when you just need to talk and get things off your chest.

Finding someone you can talk to is one way of dealing with your emotions, to let it out instead of keeping it bottled up inside.

Talking things out can feel like a huge weight has been lifted off your shoulders, especially when you seek comfort and support in the people that you care about and love.
Don't be afraid to ask for help when you feel overwhelmed, going through a challenge always feels more manageable when you've got someone you can trust to help you through it.

- **Be Patient with Yourself**

If only getting rid of anxieties could be done as easily as snapping your fingers to make everything okay.

Overcoming anxiety though is a process which takes time, and you need to prepare yourself for that to avoid frustrations along the way.
Start small by making little changes (using the techniques to overcome a negative mindset talked about above) to help you overcome one anxious thought at a time.

Be patient with yourself, it's okay to experience setbacks every now and then. Normal, even.

- **Minimize Your Caffeine Consumption**
  Coffee lovers might not be too thrilled with this coping method, but it has been proven through studies which have been conducted that caffeine is partially responsible for increasing your anxiety levels.

  You don't need to cut it out of your life completely, but if you do notice that it makes you more jittery, nervous or anxious than ever, you might need to think about cutting back on the amount of caffeine you're taking in per day.

  Other studies have shown that when taken in moderation, coffee does offer health certain health benefits. The way caffeine affects you is going to differ based on your sensitivity levels, and if it doesn't affect your anxiety levels as badly, then that's good news for you.

- **Write Down Your Worries**
  If you're not keen on keeping a journal, you could consider writing notes on your mobile phone, tablet, or laptop to write about your feelings.

You could even record a voice note if venting verbally feels better. The point is to not keep these emotions bottled up inside.

Writing can be extremely therapeutic, and when it's for your eyes alone, you're free to pour out your heart and soul, let it all flow free.

Open the floodgates and release everything that you feel and don't stop writing until you've felt much better. You don't have to be a fantastic writer either, you just need to be able to write.

- **Spend Time with People You Love**

  Having people you love around you can act as a tremendous support system when times are tough.

  Having that familiar social network that feels like home can give you a sense of belonging that just might be the comforting force you need to help you overcome your moments of anxiety, stress, and worry.

It's definitely better than going through the ordeal alone, that's for sure.

Studies have found this approach to be particularly beneficial for women, where spending time with loved ones and friends help to stimulate the release of the oxytocin hormone, which is a natural relief for stress.

The effect, according to that same study, is referred to as having the opposite effect of the fight or flight mechanism.

The findings of this study are further supported by the fact that other studies have revealed how those who didn't have as many social contacts in their lives were more susceptible to anxiety and depression.

- **Get Comfortable with Saying No**
  Sometimes, managing your anxiety and stress levels could be as simple as learning to say no to the things you don't want to do.
  Once you give up on the pursuit to make others happy at the expense of your own happiness, saying no gradually gets easier as you start to prioritize your happiness first.

If you can't take on the extra workload at the office because you've already got your hands full, it's okay to say no.

If you can't commit to a social event this weekend because you know you need some personal time to yourself and attend to your own needs, it's okay to say no.

You're not obligated to make others happy if it means compromising your own mental health and wellbeing.

Not all stress triggers are out of your control, and one effective way of managing your emotions is by learning to say "no" more.

There's no law out there that's forcing you to take on more than you can handle, so don't do it and take control of this stress trigger.

- **Take Up Meditation**
One of the most underrated forms of relaxation and mindfulness is meditation. It's not uncommon to find those who underestimate the benefits that meditation brings.

But think about this for a minute: *Meditation is a practice which has been around for decades,* and there's a very good reason why – because it *works.*

It's effective at invoking feelings of calm and relaxation, at teaching you how to breathe so you can better control your panic attacks, and meditation helps you mindfully quiet and calm your thoughts so you can get your anxieties and panic attacks under control.

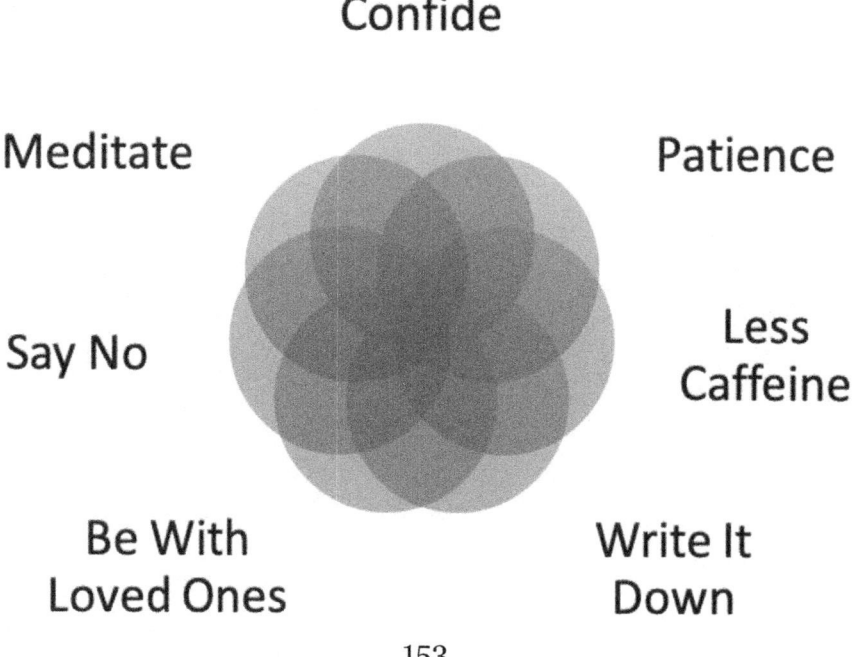

Steps to Reduce Anxiety, Stress, and Worry

Chapter 5: Master It, Control It, Be Happy About It

Jonathan Martensson summed up the essence of what it means to master your emotions in a simple quote: *"Your emotions are like the waves of the ocean. You can't stop them from coming, but you can choose which wave you want to surf"*.

Martensson's quote a profound reminder that you will never be able to prevent your emotions, but you can choose *how* you're going to let it affect you.

Every emotional experience you have undergone in your life up to this point has shaped you into the person that you are today.

The decisions that you've made, the actions you've taken (or not taken), have all been spurred in one way or another by some emotion.

There's an old saying that goes *"it's not what happens to you, but rather how you choose to respond to it that matters",* and this is true.

It is the *way* you have chosen to respond that has led you to this point in your life, where you are right now. And the *way you chose to respond* was influenced by your perception and interpretation of the circumstances that happened in your life.

When you're unable to manage your emotions properly, that's when you make impulsive decisions that often result in regret later on.

You experience emotions every day, and each emotion is there to serve a purpose.

Even the negative ones. All those emotions you would rather not feel or confront are there to help you, to give you the necessary guidance needed to make the most effective decisions.

If you were in a dead-end job that you knew was going nowhere, and you know with the skills you have, you deserve something better, without those negative emotions you feel at work, you wouldn't be motivated to take some action by searching for new jobs.

Without the frustration and unhappiness of not being valued at work, you wouldn't have that burning desire to seek out better opportunities. There would be nothing pushing you to *make the decision* to leave a job you that you know you've outgrown.

Steps to Master Your Emotions

Before you can begin with other techniques to help you master your emotions, you need to first break down the basic steps that lead up to the process:

Step 1: Begin by Identifying What Emotions You Feel

The first exercise that you can begin working to develop and improve your control over your emotions is to identify what you feel.

Observe your feelings and reflecting on them.

It is easy to fall out of touch with ourselves in this hectic world that we live in.

With the hectic lives we juggle, trying to manage one thing after another, taking care of ourselves often falls by the wayside and we lose that connection to our innermost feelings.
Instead of learning to focus on our emotions when they arise, we choose to do the easier, more convenient thing.

Either we brush it aside, ignore them or deny them completely.

Maybe we even distract ourselves from those feelings by doing something else. The more you deny your feelings though, the harder it becomes to manage them later on.

Bottling up your emotions and hoping they will just go away on its own has never proven to be an effective strategy.

If it were, there would be no such thing as emotional outbursts. From now on, whenever you experience an emotion (no matter what it may be), observe it, acknowledge it, and reflect on how it is making you feel.

> "Don't judge or analyze what you observe. Watch the thought, feel the emotion, observe the reaction. Don't make a personal problem out of them."
> — Eckhart Tolle

Step 2: Acknowledge and Appreciate

It's natural to want to resist negative emotions. They're unpleasant, but you now need to embrace them just as you would with the emotions that make you feel good.

Acknowledge that they're there, and don't fight it off. Resisting them will only diminish your confidence in your ability to remain in control, and a lack of confidence is going to work against your attempt to make progress.

Openly acknowledge that you feel the way you do, there's nothing to be ashamed of. Analyze and think about the significance of that emotion in relation to the situation that you find yourself in.

Why do you feel this way? What has triggered such a response?

When someone has made you angry for example, instead of resisting the emotion, acknowledge your anger the circumstances that triggered it.

> "Treat negative emotions like negative people. Acknowledge their presence and make whatever changes are required to remove them from your life."

Step 3: Analyze and Be Curious

Curiosity will open the door towards greater, more unique insight into your emotions and your triggers.

Curiosity will give you a better grasp of your personality and why certain circumstances have the ability to affect you in such a way.

Curiosity will lead you to analyze your emotions and ask yourself questions like *how is this emotion benefiting me?*
What am I learning about myself through this emotion?

What is the value behind this emotion?

How is it specifically serving me?

What can I do to respond better in the future?

What have I learned from this emotional experience that is going to help me grow?

Yes, every emotion serves a purpose. Even the negative ones. All our emotions are there to teach us the valuable life lessons that we need, we only need to start opening our eyes and paying attention to detail to see those lessons.

Be open to discovering the answers that you seek, and it will help you overcome the emotional roadblocks that have been holding you back all this time.

Step 4: Eliminate the "I'm A Victim" Mentality

Feeling sorry for yourself when your emotions have got out of hand is not beneficial.

Yes, you feel sorry and regret what's been done. You wish you would have handled the situation better but feeling sorry for yourself is not going to change what has happened.

Negativity will one serve to make your emotions spiral even more out of control than they already are.

Things always seem 10 times when you're down in the dumps, so it's time to get rid of this habit and start taking accountability for your emotions.

> "Feeling sorry for yourself, and your present condition, is not only a waste of energy but the worst habit you could possibly have."
>
> — Dale Carnegie

Step 5: Be Confident in Your Abilities

You can do this. Your emotions may have gotten out of control in the past, but you still have it within you remain in control, but you must believe in yourself before that can happen.

Being emotional can bring out your inner critic. We have a tendency to be hard on ourselves and we feel like we have failed in some way.

However, if you hope to master your emotions, you need to develop the confidence you need to become psychologically stronger.

Being too hard on yourself will only make your emotions more difficult to regulate because you're constantly critical and that makes your emotions fluctuate.

Reclaim your belief in yourself by thinking back to all those times in the past when you have successfully responded appropriately in an emotional situation.

You might have had your doubts back then too, but you did it anyway. Which means you can do it again.

> "Believe in yourself! Have faith in your abilities! Without a humble but reasonable confidence in your own powers you cannot be successful or happy.
>
> — Dale Carnegie

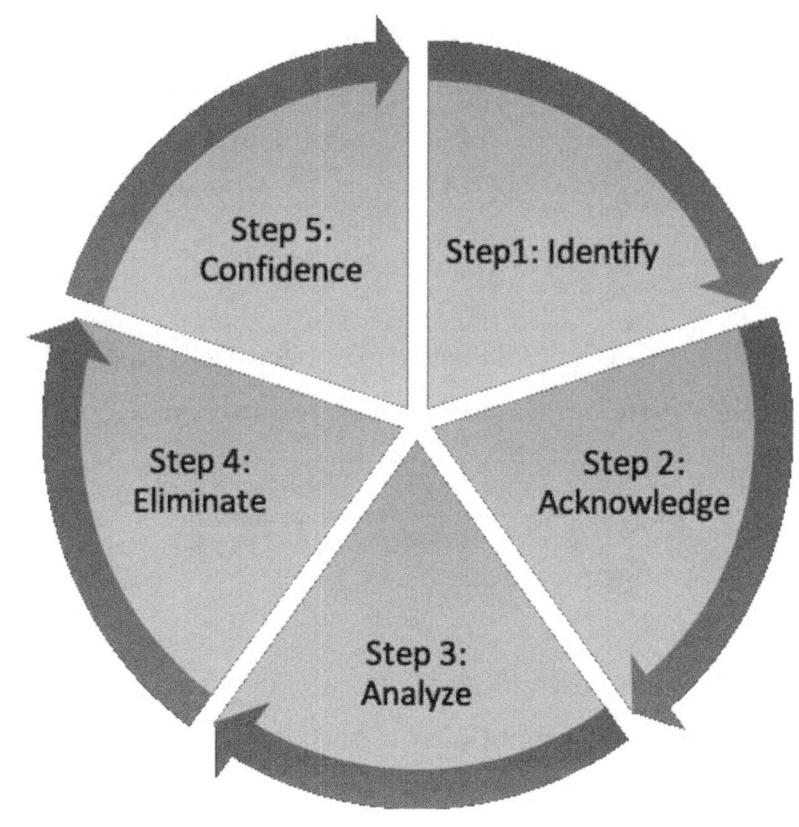

Steps to Mastering Your Emotions

Building Your Emotional Resilience

With the initial steps sorted out, it's now time to build up your emotional resilience.

Your emotions are the most persistent and present force in your life, dictating your actions, thoughts, and intentions.

Because of this, they're also the most dangerous and volatile presence in your life, and when you act on your emotions too quickly, you get into trouble.

Our emotions can fluctuate between dangerous - sometimes very dangerous - extremes. Lean too much towards one emotion and you risk putting yourself on the extreme end of that feeling. Veer too much towards irritation and you might find yourself bordering on anger or rage.

Too much of one extreme is never a good thing, and as with everything else in life, emotions are best dealt with using balance, logic, and moderation.

Regulation is the best way to avoid reacting in a way that you regret, and this is what you can do to ensure that you always react with calm and composure in almost any type of situation:

- **Avoid Reacting Immediately**
  No matter which way you spin it, impulsive reactions are almost always a mistake.

On the rare occasion that it does turn out for the best, that's pure luck and again, very rarely happens.

It's not going to be easy to fight the urge to react, but this is the time you need to dig deep and use every ounce of willpower you have left in you to pull it off.

No matter what reaction you feel like taking, always stop. Pause, breathe, consciously unclench your muscles, and keep breathing until your heart rate returns to its normal rhythm.

When you've had a moment to think about your reaction, that's usually when you realize your first impulse was not the right one to take and you'll be glad that you didn't.

- **Maintaining A Healthy Body**

A healthy mind and body is the stepping stone towards learning how to master your emotions.

You need to eat right, exercise enough and make it a habit to get regular sleep each night.

You need to be balanced on the inside before you can learn to conquer anything.

- **Develop Emotional Intelligence**

You may not have learned this kind of intelligence in school, but emotional intelligence is just as important (if not more) as academic smarts.

This is the only *real* way to fine-tune your emotions, to learn the subtle differences between each experience so you become somewhat of a sommelier when it comes to emotions.

Once your brain is able to comprehend, anticipate and categorize the sensations that you feel more accurately, you'll be able to tailor your responses and actions to suit the situation.

- **Built Resilience**

Having a better mindset will involve you working on building up your resilience.

This means that you will have to become a more determined individual, to no longer let challenges and setbacks affect you mentally and emotionally. To keep persisting even when things are difficult. Building up your resilience until you are a stronger person mentally and emotionally will help you control your anger in a way that you were never able to before.

- **Keep Checking In**

    No matter what situation you find yourself in, always remember to stop and check in with yourself.
    How am I feeling?

    Am I still able to control my emotions?

    How do I feel right now around this person or situation?

    Close your eyes and take a couple of measured deep breaths, remind yourself to focus on your present, and shift your mind away from what is threatening to trigger your emotions.

    Even when you've eventually learned how to get a good handle on your emotions, it's still good to check in with yourself every now and then.

- **Don't Shift the Blame**

    If you're always looking for an opportunity to blame someone else, to eagerly shift the blame so you don't have to feel as bad about losing control, you need to keep working on your emotional intelligence.

    That person may have provoked your emotions, but the way you chose to react was still *your decision.*

No one forced you into it, that was completely your decision and yours alone.

You need to accept partial responsibility for what happened, even if that person was at fault if they did intentionally provoke you (some people don't realize what they're doing).

A sign of someone with low emotional intelligence is a person who is always looking to shift the blame. Don't be this person because you know you are capable of being so much better than that.

- **Change Your Focus**

Whenever faced with a situation that is aggravating your emotions, try switching your focus.

Direct your attention to something else, preferably something that is going to make you feel better and immediately take your mind off what was bothering you earlier.

The more focus on the unpleasant emotion, the worse it seems to become by the minute.

We can't help it, somehow, we get sucked into the vortex of emotions, especially when they are negative ones, and they just seem to have a much stronger pull over us.

- **Find an Outlet**
  Emotions need to be released in one way or another.

  Once you've managed to control it, you need to then release it (not suppress it). Find an activity that allows you to release your emotions in a healthy manner.

  Exercise is one way of channeling your emotions in a way where no one gets hurt. The bonus there is you feel better and get fitter while you're at it. Meditation and yoga are two forms of relaxation that help you return the calm and tranquility to your mind.

  Immerse yourself in a hobby or a passion that soothes and release you.

  Keeping a journal for example, as a means of releasing your emotions instead of lashing out at others.

Painting your emotions is another approach to take. It can be any activity that makes you feel better and acts as a form of release.

As long as you can say *I feel so much better!* After you've done it, that's good enough for a start.

Make It Your Personal Commitment to Change

Having a valid reason why will help you stay on course as you work towards improving your emotions.

Why is it important for you to make this change?

Why did you decide to commit to this process?

These are questions you must be able to answer with clarity, conviction, and to remind yourself of the reason to keep going when you start to encounter obstacles along the way.

Knowing your *"Why"* is how you remind yourself to keep moving forward, and there will be many moments during this journey when you're going to need it.

Controlling your emotions is something that requires a deep commitment from you, and that commitment is going to come from your reason *why*.

Developing Self-Control to Live a Happier Life

Happiness is a result of several factors, not just one sole reason alone.

One of these contributing factors is self-control.

It is the trait that you need to help you accomplish the goals you set, to a trait that gives you the discipline to stay with the hard decisions that push your boundaries, to keep you persevering through the storms you need to come out victorious on the other side.

All of which ultimately leads to happiness.

Definition of Self-Control

Your ability to regulate and alter your predominant response is defined as self-control.

Essentially, it is your ability to manage your emotions, your feelings and the action that you take. It is your ability to delay short-term gratification (which is not something that's easy to do, admittedly), and to hold out for the bigger benefit in the long-term.

Essentially, it is the ability to sacrifice your short-term happiness for the promise of even greater happiness in the future. The sacrifice though is something that a lot of people struggle with.

Not everyone is going to be comfortable, or even have the willpower that is strong enough to resist temptation and to be able to go against your own impulses.

Unless you want something bad enough you're willing to forgo everything else, most of the time we find ourselves succumbing into temptation, only to find out that it doesn't give us the lasting happiness we were hoping to get.

Self-control is not meant to strip you of any joy by forcing you to live a more restrictive and guided life than you would like.

In fact, according to Wilhelm Hoffman in a 2013 study he conducted, it was the people with self-control who exhibited the highest levels of happiness.

They were happier because they could deal with any conflicts that came up as they worked towards achieving their goal, and self-control prevented them from indulging in behaviors which they knew were self-destructive and not beneficial.

It was self-control that held them back from making decisions based purely on impulse, and with the decisions they did make, they were happier about it because they knew it was the right thing to do.

Everyone could benefit from having some self-control instilled into their lives. The benefits you stand to gain from having a healthy dose of self-control include:

- Having that driven motivation that many people lack, which leads them to give in to their temptation to give up when they feel like it.

- Developing a better understanding of why you need to make the sacrifices you have to for the greater good.

- Being disciplined enough not to give up halfway when things get tough, and finishing what you started.
- It stops you from acting impulsively.

- It helps you keep procrastination at bay. Instead of putting off until tomorrow what you can do today, you get it done *today*. Instead of delaying your attempts to try and learn to master your emotions until "the time is right", self-control curbs that urge to procrastination and motivates you to begin *today*.

- You're less likely to give in to your temptations for the sake of instant gratification.

- It gives you the motivation you need to push your boundaries and go the extra mile. Each time you achieve a goal or a milestone through self-discipline, it gives you that boost of confidence, pride, happiness and satisfaction that you have accomplished something meaningful.

- It helps you develop positive lifestyle habits which will greatly benefit you in the long run.

- It teaches you to stay focused, despite the distractions that might try to derail you.

- It helps you get things done.
- It helps you realize you are capable of doing anything that you set your mind to.

Self-control is a behavioral trait that is learned.

It requires the breaking of bad habits and the formation of newer, better ones that improve your overall lifestyle.
Happiness follows when an effort is made to enhance your quality of life, giving you the freedom to make healthier choices instead of emotional mistakes.

You can't accomplish a goal if you aren't someone who's got a healthy dose of self-control instilled in your life.

When you feel like your life is going nowhere, it's impossible to feel happy.

Incorporate more self-control today and your future happiness will thank you for it tomorrow (not literally tomorrow, but one day).

But *Why* Is It So Hard to Develop?

You know that you need it. You know it's going to help you out.

Yet, developing the self-control and self-discipline you need feels like one of the hardest exercises to do.

If it's good for you, then *why does it have to be so hard?*

For one simple reason: *it takes effort*, and anything that requires effort is never going to be easy. If it was easy, we would all be doing it.

No, self-control is not something that is going to come easy to anybody, self-control is something that you constantly have to work hard at, and that is what makes it so difficult to hold onto.

Everyone that you see who has achieved success didn't just have it fall onto their laps.

They achieved it because they were willing to do things and make sacrifices that others were not.

They had to work hard to keep their self-control going, and they are still working hard at it every day. It's an ongoing process, one a one-time effort.

There are no shortcuts, unfortunately.

The Link Between Self-Control and Self-Esteem

Self-control isn't just linked to happiness, it's been linked to increased levels of self-esteem too.

Each time, show the ability to exercise self-control over any aspect of your life, your self-esteem and belief in yourself will be the one that reaps the benefits.

When you see the result of just how much you accomplished because you persisted despite how you were feeling, your self-esteem is given a boost, along with the belief in yourself, which eventually boosts your happiness along with it.

It reinforces in your mind that you are capable of doing this.

Every achievement that you make through self-control is going to boost your happiness and self-esteem just a little bit more, and fuel the desire to keep going, going and going.

This desire will keep fueling you forward until eventually before you know it, you're on a roll and you've become an unstoppable force.

Steps to Building Your Happiness and Self-Control

There is no one, straightforward answer in response to the question *"What can I do to be happy?"*.

That's because we are all different. No two people are going to have the exact same answer.

What constitutes happiness to you might be completely different to someone else.

As such, there is no one direct path to happiness, and there are multiple ways for you to begin the first few steps toward building your happiness and increase your self-control simultaneously:

- **Excuses Must Become a Thing of The Past**
  Excuses, excuses. They have never helped you out before, and they never will.

If you want to increase self-control and live happier, then the excuses have got to go. Right now.

If there isn't a concrete reason why you shouldn't start something, then don't look for excuses not to do it.

If there's no good reason why you shouldn't be working hard to control and master your emotions, don't create a reason to do it.

Starting is always the hardest phase of any process, but once you get into the swing of things, it only gets easier from there.

- **Go to Your Happy Place**

Think of something that happened to you which made you feel like that moment was the happiest you have ever felt in your life.

A powerful, significant memory that has stuck with you all this time—a memory so strong that it can bring a smile to your face and a rush of good feelings once more.

Focus on the rush of positive feelings that it gives you. That's going to be your anchor.

Whenever you find yourself struggling, make this anchor your go-to happy place, and let the powerful emotions from this memory infuse you with feelings of optimism and happiness.

- **Keep Expectations Realistic**
Unrealistic expectations will only kill your happiness.

Learning how to master your emotions is something that is going to happen over time because you are essentially cultivating a better version of yourself.

Building anything from scratch is always going to take time, but those who have been patient enough remain optimistic and happy throughout the process because they know that good things always take time.

- **Understand Your Weaknesses**
Weaknesses are another part of being human. Even the strongest person you know personally still has a weakness or two, a battle of their own that they're fighting.

But how these strong people continue to remain happy despite their weaknesses is because they *understand* what they are and how it affects them.

They don't pretend that their vulnerabilities and shortcomings don't exist, and they don't behave like those weaknesses don't exist.

They take accountability for them, and that gives them the ability to remain happy and maintain the self-control they need to improve.

- **Keeping Track of Your Progress**
When you can see yourself moving forward, that cements in your mind that something is happening.

Progress is taking place, and that thought encourages you to keep going.

Sometimes it's hard to look at how far you've come when you don't keep track of what you've been doing.

Tracking your progress is a visual representation that lets you see that you have indeed made progress and come a long way from where you first started.

Map out your progress, create charts, write it down, whatever works best for you that allows you to track your progress from day one is the boost of motivation that you need.

- **Change Your Routine Every Now and Then**
Shaking up your routine every now and then keeps things interesting and fresh.

Routine and monotony can get mundane after a while, even though you may love what you do.

If you're lucky, you just might stumble across something else that makes you happy too and having more elements that create happiness is always a welcomed change.

Concluding Thoughts

Admittedly, it can be hard to remain positive all the time, especially when you've experienced a setback or things are not going according to plan.

If you are going to maintain the motivation you need to keep going, it is very important that you find a way to stay positive, no matter what obstacles you may face.

There is no one-size-fits-all solution, what makes one person happy might not necessarily work for someone else.

What you could do instead is try to look at each setback as a learning opportunity and train your mind to look at this from a positive point of view.

See the bright side and the good of every situation, and you will find that happiness is easier to hold onto than it initially seems.

There is no shortcut on the road to mastering your emotions.

You have to put in the time, effort, and energy into the entire process if you want to make it happen.

You will get there eventually, but you can only *get there* if you're willing to work for it.

Your emotions will put you to the test, and push you beyond your limits, but once you learn how to control them, that's when everything starts to change.

That's when mastering of emotional intelligence starts to happen.

Conclusion

Thanks for making it through to the end of this book, let's hope it was informative and able to provide you with all of the tools you need to achieve your goals whatever they may be.

Emotions. A simple word that is capable of halting you in your tracks. To derail all the hard work you've done and set you back several steps, *only when* it gets out of control.

Opportunities can be crippled by powerful emotions like fear, worry, anger, anxiety, and stress.

They hold you back and keep you from living your dreams. But, as we've seen from everything you've learned in this book so far, learning to become the master of your emotions is entirely possible, and it *all begins with you*.

This is a journey that no one else can accomplish for you.

They may be able to offer you the guidance and support you need along the way, but only you can complete the journey and see it all the way through.

Emotions will only be a mental prison if you allow them to be. Don't be afraid to fall along the way, though—and even make mistakes, because you will never truly fail if you learn from those experiences and put that knowledge to good use as you move forward.

Finally, if you found this book useful in any way, a review on Amazon is always appreciated!

Made in the
USA
Monee, IL